The Semantic Structure of Written Communication

SIL International®

Managing Editor

Susan McQuay

Proofreader

Gene Burnham

Production Staff

Judy Benjamin, Compositor
Barbara Alber, Graphic Designer

The Semantic Structure of Written Communication

John Beekman, John Callow
Michael Kopesec

**Fifth revision, May
1981 Reprint version,
2018**

**SIL International®
Dallas, TX**

© 2018 by SIL International®
Library of Congress Catalog No: 2017945949
ISBN-978-1-55671-406-1

Copies of this and other publications of SIL International® may be obtained through distributors such as Amazon, Barnes & Noble, other worldwide distributors and, for select volumes, www.sil.org/resources/publications:

SIL International Publications
7500 W. Camp Wisdom Road
Dallas, Texas 75236-5629 USA

General inquiry: publications_intl@sil.org
Pending order inquiry: sales_intl@sil.org
www.sil.org/resources/publications

CONTENTS

PREFACE

The authors wish to express their gratitude to the many students and staff who have contributed to this volume by their helpful suggestions and critical interaction. Also we thank Bonnie Kopesec, Ida Wells, and Eleanor McAlpine, who worked many hours to prepare the manuscript for printing in time for the summer classes. Gratitude is also expressed to Bruce Moore and Alan Healey, whose significant observations on earlier versions have contributed materially to the manuscript's present form. The authors take full responsibility for any remaining errors, obscurities, etc., and would be grateful for any comments on the contents.

PART I

OVERVIEW OF THE THEORY

1

SOME BASIC NOTIONS ABOUT LANGUAGE

1.1 There Is a Fundamental Distinction Between Form and Meaning in Language

What is language? A definition which is often given is that language is "a system of communication." This is a good start towards defining language, but the definition is very broad. Another that could be given is that "language is a system of (observable) signs which communicates cognitive notions." This is preferable to the first definition, since it states what sort of system is involved and what is being communicated. But it still includes any type of observable sign, such as waving one's hand, a red traffic signal, or blowing a whistle at the end of a soccer game. If we seek to limit the definition to communication by speech, it can be further refined to "Language is a means of communication through a system of verbal signs which are based on a reciprocal relation between a perceivable signifier and a specifiable aspect of the cognitive or referential world of the communicators." By using the term *verbal*, this definition specifies that speech, rather than any other means of communication, is under consideration. At the same time, this definition needs to be more fully explained.

When verbal signs are contrasted with nonverbal signs (as used in the three illustrations above), it is implied that, regardless of the form a sign may have in communication, the fact that it is serving as a sign suggests the importance of the notion of sign in any discussion of language. What, then, is a sign? A *sign* is defined as any *form-meaning composite*. Any object, any verbal sound, any graphic representation—in short, anything that may be perceived by the senses—may serve as the form in a form-meaning composite. Form by itself, however, is not a sign; it must always have meaning to the one perceiving the form. Thus, *squilk* is a graphic form, and if it is pronounced aloud, it has phonic form, too. But it is not a sign in English, for it is not associated with any conventional meaning by English-speaking communities. Similarly, if a friend were to meet you outside your home, smile, and slap his left shoulder three times in succession with his right hand, it would be a physical form, but not a sign, since it has no recognized meaning in your common culture. Thus, a sign is only spoken of when referring to a form-meaning composite.

Note also the use of the term *reciprocal* in the above definition. There is a reciprocal relation between form and meaning in every sign. The form brings to mind that to which it refers by conventional association; conversely, conceptualization of a referent brings to mind the form or forms conventionally associated with it. Without this reciprocal relationship, there would be no form-meaning composite. In particular, therefore, every sign used in language exhibits this form-meaning reciprocity.

The sorts of signs used in language are known as *symbols*. The term symbol is used of signs where the association between the form of the sign and its meaning is an arbitrary one; that is to say, there is no direct physical or natural association. For example, there is a physical association between a green arrow pointing to the left and its meaning "traffic turning left may now go." The direction is the same. On the other hand, there is no such association between the meaning "you may now go" and the color green, so that the use of green in traffic signals is said to be "arbitrary." Similarly, the fact that English uses the word *house*, French the word *maison*, and Spanish *casa* to refer to a certain class of objects, is, in this technical sense, also arbitrary. So language signs belong to the subclass of signs known as symbols. (Cf. Spradley 1972); if longer citation is desired, it should be (Cf. Spradley, James P. 1972. Foundations of cultural knowledge. In James P. Spradley (ed.), Culture and cognition: Rules, maps and plans. San Francisco, California: Chandler Publishing Co.)

With this understanding of what a sign is, we can now return to the question of identifying the major components of language. To acknowledge that verbal signs are an essential feature of all languages is at the same time to acknowledge that language is a composite of form and meaning. Since a sign is a composite of form and meaning and since language is a system of verbal signs, we therefore conclude that language is a composite of form and meaning. Both of these major components of language must form part of any adequate study of a specific language or of language in general.

1.2 The Primary Dimensions of Form

The definition given above can be restated as follows: "Language is a means of communication based upon a reciprocal relation between sounds and cognition." Here, the form-meaning composite is more specifically named as a reciprocal relationship between systematically structured sounds and intended meaning. Spoken communication is dependent upon sound—not just random sounds, but a selection of sounds from the total range of sounds that a human being is capable of producing. These sounds are structured into such units as phonemes, syllables, phonological words, and larger groupings. These sounds may also be analyzed as to which sounds are contrastively significant in the formation of verbal signs. This presents a somewhat simplified description of the *phonological structure* of language.

These same sounds may be analyzed as to what combinations of them correspond with different cognitive concepts. A list of these combinations of sounds represents the *lexicon* of a language. The lexicon is the formal set of sound combinations used to symbolize those segments of the referential world which the language group, with its particular interests, emphases, etc., chooses to identify and talk about. Each such segmentation is manifested in various contrastive phonological shapes. Thus, the lexicon is the organization of sounds to symbolize different cognitive notions.

Yet again, these same sounds may be analyzed as to how the lexical items are arranged and modified to form the various grammatical units such as words, phrases, clauses, and sentences. This is referred to as the *grammar* of a language, which orders and hierarchically organizes the lexicon into grammatical units. The patterns by which a specific language represents information are referred to as its grammar and lexicon. Both the lexicon and the grammar are formal systems which serve a single purpose, namely, to communicate information through the use of symbols.

These features of language, i.e., the speech sounds in their phonological, lexical, and grammatical structures, constitute the *form* of a language. They are the essential, formal dimensions of any language, which may be referred to as its *surface structure*. The surface structure serves to give perceptible substance to cognitive notions. Thought can only be shared with others by giving it perceptual shape. This is what sound does—not just any sound, but sound that is phonologically, lexically, and grammatically structured.

Language, then, has two major components, form and meaning. The dimensions of form have already been named—the phonological, lexical, and grammatical structures of sounds. With this brief discussion of the form of language, we are now ready to look at meaning in more detail.

1.3 The Primary Dimensions of Meaning

As is true with form, so also meaning is multidimensional. In the theory presented here, we recognize three aspects of meaning: referential, situational, and structural. Each of these correlates with a particular part of the overall communication event, as shown by figure 1.1. The whole represents

COMMUNICATION EVENT

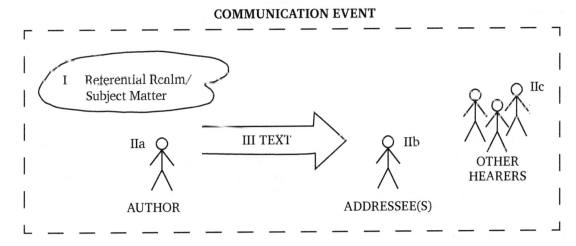

Figure 1.1. The parts of the communication event.

the communication event, and the three numbered items represent the parts of the communication event to which the three aspects of meaning correlate. One important part of the communication event has to do with what the communication is about (I)—i.e., the subject matter, or often what is called the "referential realm." Information in a discourse that correlates directly with some aspect of the referential realm is *referential meaning*.

Another important part of the communication event is that which pertains to its participants and the situation in which the communication takes place (IIa–c). (Note that the participants of the communication situation (II) must be distinguished from those of the referential realm (I). However, it is possible for the participants of the communication situation and those involved in the subject matter to be the same, for example, when the communication situation participants are talking about themselves.) Much of the information communicated by a discourse can be accounted for only by correlating it with features of the communication situation (both the participants and their setting or context). Such information is called *situational meaning*.

Another part of the communication event that is needed to account for the meaning of a discourse is the information structure of the discourse itself (III); that is, how the information bits are "packaged" and how these units are related to one another within the discourse structure. Information of this nature is *structural meaning*.

1.3.1 Referential meaning

Although there are three distinct aspects of meaning, it is important to realize that the three occur simultaneously in any discourse or part of a discourse. Whether a given bit of information in a particular part of a discourse is referential, situational, or structural may be determined by asking the question, "With which of the three general parts of the communication event can that bit of information be correlated?" Consider, for example, the sentence, "Bill hit the ball." Although this sentence is short and simple, it does contain a lot of information and can illustrate quite nicely what is referential meaning as distinguished from situational and structural meaning.

Much of the information communicated by this sentence is referential. The word "Bill" communicates at least the following referential components of meaning: male human being named "Bill," likely beyond the toddler stage. The word "ball" communicates at least the following referential information: a relatively small, spherical thing, generally used as an object of play. The word "hit" communicates an action, most likely involving the use of an instrument (bat, racket, etc.). Furthermore, the arrangement of the three words clearly indicates that the referent "Bill" is functioning as the Agent (the animate doer) of the action, and the referent "ball" is the Affectant (that which is affected) of the action. All of this information is referential in the sense that it correlates with and is accounted for by aspects of the referential realm of the communication event.

But there is information communicated to us by this sentence that is not referential. Notice, for instance, that the sentence is in the past tense. There is nothing in the referential realm per se that can account for the tense. Such information has to be accounted for either by reference to situational factors of the communication event or by reference to structural aspects of the discourse itself. Notice also that grammatically the sentence is indicative; that is, it makes an assertion. Once again, there is nothing in the referential realm that can account for this modal or illocutionary information. Once again, it is by reference to the situational aspects of the communication event (i.e., the author's intentions) that such information can be accounted for.

Furthermore, that Bill (the Agent of the action hit) occurs as the grammatical "subject" of the sentence communicates to us some information that is not referential. It cannot be correlated with anything in the referential realm; rather, it must be accounted for by correlating it with the information structure. In this case, "Bill" appears to be the "topic" at this particular point of the discourse of which the sample sentence is a part. The fact that the instrument was not explicitly mentioned, communicates either that the author is assuming that the addressees know this information (i.e., situational meaning—author's presupposition); or that the information is structurally presupposed (i.e., structural meaning—old information) or is structurally nonprominent (i.e., structural meaning—information focus).

1.3.2 Situational meaning

All communication takes place in a situational context, in what may be termed a *communication situation*. Usually, within the general situation, there are specific aspects of it which constrain the author to compose his particular message. The implication of this is that many features of the communication situation will be reflected in the message. Put the other way around, in studying the surface structure form, some of the meaning signaled by it will reflect and correlate with the situation in which the communication was composed. Such components of meaning are called *situational meaning*.

The component features of situational meaning. Situational meaning can be briefly defined as information that correlates with the relation between the surface structure and various features of the communication situation. Thus, situational meaning is accounted for by features that are external to the discourse itself which influence, directly and indirectly, many of the choices the author makes as he composes his discourse. Some of these external factors may be referred to in the discourse explicitly; others may need to be deduced.

Consider, for example, the phrase "my dear brothers" used by James several times in his epistle (1:16, 19; 2:5; etc.). When he uses this phrase, he communicates to us that there was a group, or more probably a number of groups of believers, to whom he could write, and that he regarded them with Christian affection. In other words, it is possible for the person studying the surface structure to reconstruct, to some extent, the situation in which (and, perhaps, because of which) the author wrote.

Figure 1.2 provides a summary of components of the communication situation that may significantly affect the information content and structure of a discourse.

AUTHOR	ADDRESSEE(S)	MESSAGE
TIME	TIME	TIME (of the reported content in relation to the time when the message was given)
LOCATION	LOCATION	LOCATION (of the reported content in relation to the location of the author and/or addressees)
SOCIAL STATUS	SOCIAL STATUS	CULTURAL SETTING (ecological, sociological, technological, and cognitive aspects)
PRESUPPOSITIONS		OCCASION
RELATIONSHIP		MEDIUM

Figure 1.2. Situational aspects of a communication event.

In the left-hand column of figure 1.2, *time* refers to the period during which the author and addressee(s) lived, and where possible, more specifically to the date that the composition took place. *Location* refers to the general location of the author and addressee(s) and the more specific location within the general. Thus, a city might be named as the general location and a particular place within the city as a more specific location. For example, Paul is generally considered to have written Ephesians, Philippians, Colossians, and Philemon from the city of Rome and, more specifically, from a prison somewhere in that city. *Social status* refers to such matters as age, educational background, position in the social structure, etc. *Presuppositions* refer to the author's knowledge, beliefs, and attitudes with reference to the subject matter, and also his assumptions about the addressee's knowledge, beliefs, and attitudes with reference to the subject matter. *Relationship* is placed in the center, since it refers to the mutual relationships between the author and the addressee(s). This includes their relative positions, such as employer-employee, teacher-pupil, husband-wife, child-parent, etc.; and also the intimacy of that relationship, from very close to definitely antagonistic, with unacquainted as a mid-point on the scale.

In the right-hand column of figure 1.2, *time* refers to the relationship between the time of the events reported in the message and the actual time of composition (if either of these is known); and *location* is understood similarly. The *cultural setting* is divided into the following four aspects:

1. *Ecological*, which includes physical environment, climate, topography, flora, fauna, etc.:
2. *Sociological*, which includes institutions, educational system, social stratification, politics, historical experience, economics, etc.;
3. *Technological*, which covers the general level of material culture, state of science and technical knowledge, industry, agricultural interests, etc.;
4. *Cognitive*, which refers to political and religious beliefs and traditions, general values, etc.

Occasion refers to that particular set of events to which the author responded by composing his message. Broadly speaking, the *medium* may be oral or written. In the present work, we are mainly concerned with the written medium; but even within a written medium a distinction can be drawn between a literary style as opposed to a direct reflection of oral style, and a message that is written to be read aloud in public, as opposed to one that is written simply to be read privately.

The total communication situation embraces all the circumstances in which a message occurs. For practical purposes, in connection with written materials, the total communication situation can be limited to those factors which are known or presupposed as known by both the original author and the original reader(s). An author has no need, in general, to include information that is common knowledge between himself and the intended reader(s). Authors, however, do include such information in written documents. In the context of the Bible, this fact is of considerable help to us, since without some of this background information, the interpretational task would become that much more difficult. Probably the pedagogical necessity of beginning with some known information before moving into the unknown makes it a practical necessity or at least desirable, from a communication perspective, to include some information that is known to both author and intended readers.

The broad statement as to what the communication situation embraces can also be limited further by recognizing that much of the communication situation which is unknown to the addressee is also irrelevant to the purpose of the author. For example, if, while the author composed his discourse, there happened to be a dog and cat fight within earshot, this factor in the communication situation may have caused the author to pause or even delay work, but this would be a kind of situational factor that is irrelevant. Those factors in the communication situation which help us to better understand the information in the discourse are those which are relevant; and highly significant are those factors which enable the analyst to determine the *purpose* of the communication. Within the total communication situation, there will be one or more factors which constrained the author to compose the message, so that the author's purpose is closely related to specific aspects of the total communication situation.

It is all very well, however, to establish questions concerning the situational aspects involved in a communication; but when we are faced with a written discourse composed many centuries ago and essentially all we have is the surface-structure form of the document, what can be done to reconstruct the communication situation? It would seem that here an understanding of the culture of the area, as much as can be gained from materials available, is essential. Then, when looking at specific stretches of text from a clause to a paragraph, it may be possible to reconstruct some of the communication situation by asking: "What kind of a person would say this?" "Under what circumstances would this be used?"

"To whom would it likely be said?" And then perhaps a further question could be asked; namely, "Why would a person say this in a given situation?"

As we analyze Scripture, there is no member of the original communication situation available for us to question concerning what the original situation was. We must select probable situations compatible with the content of the document. Those situations which best account for the total information under analysis are to be considered the most probable and therefore the basis for choosing between interpretational options.

1.3.3 Structural meaning

As has previously been mentioned, structural meaning has to do with information that correlates with and is accounted for by the information structure of the discourse itself in the communication event. Semantic units and their interrelationships, structural types (hierarchical, string, "spiral," etc.), topic-comment (old versus new information, Functional Sentence Perspective, etc.), pronominalization, "cohesion" (a la Halliday and Hasan 1976), etc., are matters considered to come under this rubric.

Compare the following two sentences:

> (A) "Bill hit the ball."
> (B) "It was hit by him."

Both of these sentences have essentially the same components of referential meaning—"Bill" as Agent and "ball" as Affectant of the Action "hit," using some Instrument. Also, both of the sentences have essentially the same components of situational meaning—the speaker's intention to make an assertion about an event, the time of the referential event being prior to the time of the communication event, etc. However, the sentences are radically different. These differences have to do with the structure of the supposed discourse. That is, for example, what the particular part of the discourse is about—in the case of sentence (A), it is about "Bill," whereas in the case of sentence (B), it is about the "ball." Also, structurally old versus structurally new information appears to be involved in accounting for the differences between the two sentences. The use of the pronouns in sentence (B) communicates to the addressee that the two referents, the ball and Bill, were previously introduced in the discourse, i.e., they are structurally old, or known, information.

There is indeed much more that could be said concerning the nature of the three kinds of meaning. These comments, however, should suffice to introduce and distinguish them.

1.4 The Meaning Determines the Form

It has been argued that there is a distinction between form and meaning, and that the meaning conveyed by the form, or surface structure, can be looked at from three perspectives—that of the message that the author sought to communicate, that of the communication situation in which the discourse was composed by the author, and that of the information structure of the discourse itself. Relating these three aspects, some specific factors within the total situation moved the author to communicate. Having decided to communicate, he chooses an appropriate way to express what he wants to say. He may, for instance, telephone the addressee, write a letter, pen a treatise (cf. Hebrews and Martin Luther's "theses"), prepare a lecture or speech, he may compose a biography, a novel, etc. Within this larger choice, he chooses an appropriate "tone"—he may argue, he may threaten, he may take a conciliatory approach, or he may take a more neutral tone, and simply inform without marked emotional overtones. Then, having decided on his general approach, he decides what he wishes to say, organizes it (to a greater or lesser degree), and then actually presents it to his readers in a lineal manner.

Looked at in this way, it is clear that *what* the author intends to say, the meaning, takes precedence over how he says it, the form. Or put slightly differently, it is the meaning that determines the form. It is the meaning that is the essence of all communication.

Of course, it is true that meaning is communicated (in language) only by means of perceptual form, i.e., surface structure. As translators, we are very aware of this. What we begin with is a discourse represented in the surface form of certain languages—e.g., Greek, Hebrew, Aramaic (in the case of Bible translation). From this surface form we have to "decode" the meaning. Then we seek to re-express that meaning in another surface form, usually quite different from the first. From the standpoint of communication (including translation), meaning is very important. In the translation process, the translator derives meaning and its structure from the surface structure of one language and renders this back again into the surface structure of another language.

1.5 Meaning is Structured

It is more or less taken as axiomatic that (surface) form is structured; that is to say, it is amenable to the general scientific approach of observing surface forms, making hypotheses concerning them, checking these hypotheses against the linguistic data, revising them, and eventually propounding a theory that aims to account for the phenomena under study. Phonology, grammar, and lexicon have already been subjected to such studies for many years.

But what about meaning? Is it also amenable to general scientific analysis? Or is it an inaccessible, amorphous mass beyond the reach of such an approach? The assumption underlying this work is that meaning is also structured, and that this structure is amenable to linguistic analysis and theory. Indeed, the purpose of this presentation is to set forth a theory of the structure of meaning—to give it a technical title, *semantic structure*.

1.5.1 Semantic structure and surface structure

A very natural question arises at this point—does semantic structure bear any resemblance to surface structure? The answer is yes and no: yes, because both make use of such structural notions as unit, nucleus versus periphery, and hierarchy; no, because surface structure is language specific, whereas semantic structure is near universal—its features, relations, and functions being essentially the same in all languages. Or, to put it in another way: if a given written document is translated (well) into several unrelated languages, and the original and the translations are then analyzed to arrive at the semantic structure underlying the different surface forms, then the units, and their relationships, will be virtually the same. The units will show the same nuclei and peripheries, the same internal coherence, etc. (For an interesting example of this, see Takashi Manabe's (1978) comparison of the semantic structure analysis of the Greek original of a New Testament passage, and its Japanese translation. It is not insignificant, either, that the model used for the semantic analysis is not the same (though there are similarities) with that presented in this paper.)

One other observation is worth making at this point. Although it is the case that each language has its own unique surface structure, nevertheless certain surface forms, such as the finite form of the verb, are found in all languages. It seems reasonable to assume that such universal forms directly reflect the semantic structure.

1.5.2 Meaning is "packaged"

The human mind cannot handle large quantities of information unless it applies the "packaging" principle. An interesting study was done by George Miller (1956) in which he notes that the mind imposes an organizational structure on information to facilitate memory and comprehension. He observed that the mind tends to organize in groupings of *seven*. The number seven is a mean rather than an absolute, so that there are occasions when the number of items combined into an organizational package may be a few less, or, in some cases, a few more, than seven. There is, then, an *organizational* or *packaging principle* which must be reckoned with in any adequate understanding of semantic structure.

A corollary principle to the observation made by Miller brings hierarchy into consideration. As information accumulates, smaller units, ranging in number from three to nine, will be combined to form a larger unit. When the number of these larger units reaches a number between three and nine, they in turn must be combined, and so the hierarchical process becomes essential to an understanding of language and an analysis of the structure of communication.

A further and equally important observation relates to the fact that the choice of which bits and how many bits of information are combined is not arbitrary; it is not mechanically determined. If it were, one might expect that the number seven would be an absolute rather than an average. It would seem that there are certain general characteristics of the mind which are shared by all people and which determine when a quantity of information has reached a point at which it should be organized into separate packages rather than to continue on. The principles which apply universally in determining how much information will be packaged into an organizational unit before another one is started involve the notions of *unity, coherence,* and *prominence.*

As one looks upon nature (the handiwork of God), there are *units* related in a *coherent* way and having relative *prominence.* Items in one's environment are combined and grouped logically according to one's view of the world. For example, John Ruskin, in his article on composition (in Kuist 1947:13), suggests that a sprig of leaves is so organized as to exhibit unity, coherence, and prominence. He suggests, in different terms, that these features are present in all of nature. Take, for example, an individual leaf, rather than a sprig. It has "unity" in the sense that it is a whole made up of constituents (plant cells). It has "coherence" in the sense that the plant cells of which it consists are all appropriate to a leaf. If it were possible to arrange millions of cells, drawn from all sorts of creatures, in an identical shape to the leaf, it would not be a leaf, because the cells would not be leaf cells. Its coherence is also shown by the intricate network of veins relating all the cells to one another and to the stem of the leaf. It has "prominence" in the sense that among the network of veins there is a central vein to which, ultimately, all the other veins are attached. There is also prominence shown in connection with the periphery of the leaf, where there is generally a prominent point opposite to the point of attachment to the stem.

In man's artifacts, these same features of unity, coherence, and prominence can also be seen, and indeed, are often taught (though often using other labels) in such subjects as painting, music, and sculpture.

It seems reasonable to assume, then, that unity, coherence, and prominence reflect inherent categories of the human mind and so predetermine what a normal mind will produce. We can expect the artifacts of man, his games, his ceremonial activities, and his speech to be characterized by unity, coherence, and prominence. They really represent predetermining factors which influence man toward using these three categories in anything he produces. They represent the prototype in abstraction of anything that man may produce, the fountainhead which will be reflected downstream.

2

CHARACTERISTICS OF SEMANTIC STRUCTURE

Having established certain basic notions about communication by means of language, we can now turn to present an outline of the sort of semantic theory that is built on them, i.e., we can delineate its characteristics. It will be seen that these characteristics are closely related to the notions in chapter 1.

2.1 Semantic Structure Consists of Units

That units constitute an inherent feature of semantic structure follows from the premise that the mind needs to "package" information if it is to communicate or understand efficiently. Three basic units are posited for semantic structure: the *concept*, the *proposition*, and the *propositional configuration*.

2.1.1 The concept

The concept is based on the universal practice of isolating segments of the referential realm, or of circumscribing groupings of information about which one wants to communicate. The segments or groupings may be analyzed into semantic features or bits of information called *components of meaning* (Beekman and Callow 1974:67–93; Nida 1975:32–67). These language- or culture-specific "bundles" of components, i.e., concepts, may be categorized into four universal classes: Things (T), Events (E), Attributes (A), and Relations (R).

Many concepts are given "names," i.e., they are "lexicalized" (see sections 5.1 and 5.4). The collection of such concepts constitutes the *lexicon* of the language. Since concepts are virtually infinite in number, most of them are not lexicalized. Nevertheless, given the resources of the language, it is possible for an author to identify any concept he wishes to talk about. Units so isolated are called "discourse concepts" or, more simply, "concepts." They function as constituents of propositions. Often a concept will be expressed by a single word in the surface structure. When a single word does not adequately communicate that to which the author desires to refer, he then can add a word, a phrase, or even a clause until he has adequately isolated the information about which he wants to communicate. Such combinations of words are likewise functioning to represent concepts. However, since such "constructed" concepts are themselves composed of concepts, they are sometimes called "concept clusters." Consider the following sentences:

> *The kitten* played with me.
> *Three cute little kittens* played with me.
> *The kitten that belongs to Uncle Henry* played with me.

In all three examples, the italicized portion represents a single semantic unit which identifies the participant that did the action. They illustrate the flexible nature of the discourse concept.

This universal practice of using a lexicalized concept or a combination of them to identify a discourse concept illustrates what can be called *language economy*. It would be a rather impossible task for a language to have an inventory in lexical items of all the concepts which its users may want to refer to in the course of conversing or writing. For example, "boy" represents a very common concept found throughout different languages. However, languages do not generally have separate words for more specific references to a boy, such as a fat boy, thin boy, ambitious boy, tall boy, short boy, boy who is swimming, boy who is working, boy who is fighting, boy who is blind, etc. In other words, languages provide words which represent those concepts which most frequently enter into their conversations and allow for the organizational principle of packaging to fulfill the need of referring to other, more specifically defined concepts by grouping the lexicalized concepts into clusters. These clusters are represented by various surface structure forms, but still accomplish the same basic function as a single word might, i.e., to represent a concept. This principle of language economy applies not only at the level of concepts but also at higher levels.

2.1.2 The proposition

Obviously, a communicator is not content just to identify concepts. He is interested in combining these concepts in order to communicate something about them. He may want to tell of an *action* that he completed ("I gave a book to Mary"), an *experience* he had ("I tasted the delicious sauce"), a *process* ("The milk became sour"), or a *state* ("You are very tall"). Notice that in terms of their referential content, these four expressions are quite different. On the other hand, considered situationally, they are very much alike—i.e., they all make a statement. All could be converted into a command or a prohibition; all could be converted into a question. This gives a total of three different general functions which a simple combination of concepts may fulfill; *statements, commands,* and *questions.* These functions are known as *illocutionary* functions or *speech acts* (Searle 1969).

A combination of concepts which communicates an action, experience, process, or state, using one of the illocutionary functions, is called a *proposition.* It opens up to the communicator a whole range of subjects and ideas about which he may communicate. In fact, a single proposition may suffice to communicate fully everything that a communicator may want to state.

2.1.3 The propositional configuration

As is often the case, the communicator may want to give further information concerning something he has just said; so he may add a second, a third, or more propositions to help explain the first one, or back it up by arguments, or clarify it by comparing it with something else, etc. In fact, there is, in one sense, no end to this process. The communicator may go on as long as he chooses, until he has communicated all he wishes to—it may even be a book by the time he has finished! But, no matter how long it may be, what he says still consists of propositions related to one another in various ways—no further basic units are used.

This highlights the fact that communication is by nature *recursive* (i.e., units of one type cluster together to form a unit of the same type). Two propositions may be combined, then this pair may be used (for example) to explain a third, and then those three may provide an argument for a fourth, and so on. Philemon 13 (somewhat adapted) illustrates recursion (see figure 2.1).

PROPOSITIONAL CONFIGURATIONS   **PROPOSITIONS**

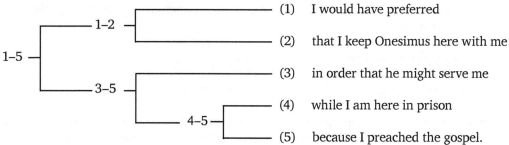

(1)   I would have preferred

(2)   that I keep Onesimus here with me

(3)   in order that he might serve me

(4)   while I am here in prison

(5)   because I preached the gospel.

Figure 2.1. Recursive structure of Philemon 13.

There are five propositions and four propositional configurations in Phlm. 13. Working from the bottom up, it can be seen that 5 gives a reason why Paul was in prison, which is 4. This pair of propositions (i.e., propositional configuration), 4–5, states the time during which Onesimus would have served Paul, which is 3. Then propositional configuration 3–5 functions as the purpose Paul had in mind for preferring to keep Onesimus, which is propositional configuration 1–2. Finally, proposition 2 states what it is that Paul would have preferred, which is 1. Recursion is seen in that propositional configuration 1–5 has two constituents, both of which are propositional configurations (1–2 and 3–5); and propositional configuration 3–5 has two constituents, one of which is a propositional configuration 4–5.

2.1.4 The concept, the proposition, and the configuration compared

Each of these units is distinctive in its structure. Not only is there a difference in how much information is packaged in each of the three units, but the constituents of each are related to one another through three distinctive systems of relations. The components of meaning within a concept are related by *delimitational relations*; the concepts within a proposition are related by *interconcept relations*, which are commonly called "case roles"; the propositions within a propositional configuration are related by *communication relations*. The relations within these three semantic units are universal, or near-universal, in all languages.

In addition to these differences, there are also differences of function. The concept is a *referring* unit, identifying segments of the referential world of the communication event; the proposition and the configuration, however, are *communication* units, since they not only name things, events, attributes, and relations, but interrelate them in purposive communicative (speech, or social) acts. These differences are shown in figure 2.2.

	CONSTITUENTS	RELATION	FUNCTION
CONCEPT	components	delimitational	to refer
PROPOSITION	concepts	case	to communicate
CONFIGURATION	propositions	communication	to communicate

Figure 2.2. The differences between the concept, proposition, and configuration.

2.2 Semantic Structure is Hierarchically Organized

It is true that all semantic units are classifiable as one of the three basic types, i.e., concepts, propositions, and propositional configurations. However, the picture is not yet complete. Because of the "packaging" principle, groups of propositional configurations are formed into units, characterized by the three semantic features of constituency (unity), coherence, and prominence; and these units are organized into a hierarchical system. The smallest unit in the hierarchy of propositional configurations is called the *propositional cluster*; the next larger unit is the *paragraph*. These are found in all types of longer discourses. Paragraphs can then be combined into larger units, and these in turn combined into yet larger ones. These "higher-level units" are labeled according to the type of communication (or discourse) in which they are found. Thus, in discourses such as the New Testament letters, paragraphs combine to form *sections* and sections, *divisions*. In narrative discourse, such as the Gospels and Acts, paragraphs often combine to form *episodes*, and episodes, *scenes*.

There is thus a semantic hierarchy of concept, proposition, propositional cluster, paragraph, etc. It will be seen immediately that the units are not the same as in the grammatical hierarchy (Longacre 1976:306). If it is assumed, for the moment, that semantic and grammatical paragraphs roughly correspond to each other (i.e., a semantic paragraph will often be represented by a surface paragraph), then the two hierarchies up to the paragraph level can be compared, as in figure 2.3. (The question of the relationship between the two hierarchies is discussed later.)

SEMANTIC HIERARCHY	GRAMMATICAL HIERARCHY
	discourse
	. . .
configuration	paragraph
	sentence
proposition	clause
	phrase
concept	word
	morpheme

Figure 2.3. The semantic and grammatical hierarchies compared.

2.3 Each Semantic Unit Has the Same Meaning Features

Each semantic unit, whether a concept, a proposition, or a propositional configuration, shows the same set of meaning features. For convenience of discussion, these are shown diagrammatically in figure 2.4. A semantic unit can be looked at from two perspectives: it can be taken apart and studied internally, or it can be taken as a whole and its function in the wider contexts of the discourse and the communication situation studied, i.e., it can be looked at externally. The *analytical* features correspond to the internal perspective; the *holistic* features correspond to the external perspective.

ANALYTICAL FEATURES	**UNITY:** Units are composed of units.	**INTERNAL COHERENCE:** Constituents are compatible and appropriately related.	**PROMINENCE:** One (or more) constituent(s) is more significant than the others.
HOLISTIC FEATURES	**CLASS:** Units are classifiable by referential, situational, and/or structural type.	**EXTERNAL COHERENCE:** Units distribute in a compatible and appropriate way and play a specifiable role in another unit.	**THEMATIC CONTENT:** Units convey prominent content to accomplish a specifiable purpose.

Figure 2.4. The meaning features of semantic units.

2.3.1 The analytical features of semantic units

As pointed out earlier in this paper, it is primarily the analytical features that characterize a unit as a unit. Put the other way around, if a stretch of written discourse lacks any of these features, then it is not a semantic unit. They are particularly important when it comes to identifying units larger than the proposition—proposition clusters, paragraphs, etc.—but they are also characteristic of the concept and the proposition.

a. *Unity.* Every semantic unit is characterized by the analytical feature of unity (constituency). By this is meant that the unit will be conceptualized as a whole which itself consists of other identifiable and isolatable semantic units. Most often the constituents of a unit at one hierarchical level will be those of the next lower level of the hierarchy. That is, the constituents of a section most characteristically are paragraphs; those of the paragraph, propositional clusters; those of the proposition, concepts; and so on. However, because of the principles of recursion (section 2.1.3) and language economy (section 2.1.1), the constituents of a unit may consist of a combination of units of the same level or lower in the semantic hierarchy. For example, a section may consist of a combination of paragraphs, propositional clusters, and propositions. Furthermore, some of the paragraphs in a section may be grouped together as quasi-sections, or "paragraph clusters."

The feature of unity may be viewed from the perspective of each of the three aspects of meaning. For example, the information communicated by a sentence may be analyzed into referential units—e.g., the Event or State and the "participants" related to it. The unit may be analyzed into situational constituents—e.g., illocution indicators, temporal indicators, emotive indicators, etc. Then, too, the unit may be analyzed into its structural constituents—e.g., topic and comment.

b. *Internal coherence.* The second analytical feature of a semantic unit is that of coherence (or compatibility). In general, by coherence is meant that the constituents of a unit will be semantically compatible with one another. Corresponding to the three subclasses of constituents of a unit, it is expected that a well-formed unit will have referential coherence, situational coherence, and structural (relational) coherence.

The first of these, *referential coherence*, has to do with the "sameness of reference" between the constituents of the unit. You cannot talk about totally diverse things if you are going to have a unit. In a semantic unit with coherence, there will always be redundancy of referential information and/or the recurrence of information belonging to the same semantic or experiential domain. There may be obvious *recurrences* of referential information through such means as repetition, the use of synonyms (i.e., words or expressions with the same meaning in the particular context), anaphora and cataphora (referring back and referring forward respectively), overlay structures (a form of repetition in which the information follows such patterns as abc, cde, efg, etc.), referential parallels, sandwich structures or *inclusio* (in which the opening and closing information is substantially the same, though not necessarily the same in form), chiastic structures (abba, abcba, etc.), and other devices.

Referential coherence also occurs when items from the same *semantic domain* are referred to. In this category there would be such obvious associations as hoe, rake, plow, seeds, wheat, to plant, and to sow. All of these belong to the domain of "farming." *Experiential domains* are more relevant in smaller units than in larger ones. For example, boy, home, and bus have no significant referential components in common, but they form an experiential domain in the sentence "The boy went home on the bus." These words, brought together in a proposition, have a degree of compatibility that makes it possible to conceptualize them as forming a single unit. However, it is very unlikely that a fully developed paragraph will only be held together by items belonging to experiential domains.

Situational coherence will characterize a semantic unit also. Concepts and the words that represent them not only refer, but they also carry emotive overtones, either positive (e.g., hero, victor, exciting), negative (jealous, rat, boring), or neutral (most words). In any given unit, there must be "connotational" coherence—the author cannot, for example, be angry and pleased at the same time in the unit (though successive units could be differentiated by change of connotational coherence). The "tone," the emotive overtones of a given unit, must cohere. Furthermore, propositions and propositional configurations have situational content as well as referential content. That is, a well-formed semantic unit should exhibit a degree of illocutionary continuity. For instance, a stretch of text may be characterized as imperative or hortatory because of the repeated occurrence of propositions with the illocutionary perspective of command; whereas other segments of the discourse would be characterized as expository because of the high frequency of occurrence of propositions with the illocutionary perspective of statement. Connotational coherence and illocutionary (functional) coherence form part of the situational coherence of a unit.

Structural coherence (or relational coherence) consists in proper relationships between the parts that make up a unit. There must be appropriateness of relation, i.e., the relationships must be compatible with the information that is being related. The combination of the particular parts and the relationship that is indicated between them must match some part of the receptor's experience or some situation that he can readily conceive of in the real world (or even in an imaginary world).

Collocational compatibility is an aspect of structural coherence, not, as might be expected, of referential coherence. Semantic domains are distinct from the relational appropriateness of collocational compatibility. Consider an earlier example. It was suggested that the words "to plant," "rake," "hoe," "sow," and "wheat" were in the same semantic domain. However, "sow" and "rake" do not collocate, in the sense that one does not "sow a rake." In other words, items in a semantic domain may not be collocationally appropriate for one another, but they may occur in a stretch of text and, by virtue of belonging to a particular semantic category of thought, give referential coherence to that particular unit. In a semantic unit with structural coherence, the parts of that unit are appropriately related to one another. In other words, the relations used are compatible with the limitations imposed by the referential content. When structural coherence exists, the referential content and the relations entered into by that referential content are appropriate and compatible.

Consider Joos's illustrative sentence (Joos 1957:15) "I have never heard a green horse smoke a dozen oranges." This sentence clearly lacks structural coherence. Grammatically, the sentence is perfectly correct, but semantically it is all askew. That is, the concepts used are inappropriate for the role that they have in the sentence. In the normal referential world, the real world in which we live (although other worlds can be invented), horses do not smoke. There is an inappropriateness of the concept "horse" for the relationship of Agent to the action "smoke." There are classes of entities that do smoke— people, for example—but not horses. The class would also include chimneys, etc. However, whatever smokes would not smoke oranges. So there is an inappropriateness of the concept serving as Affectant of the Event concept. Pipes or cigarettes, etc., might be smoked, but not oranges. Similarly, there is a problem with "I never *heard* a green horse smoke"; we do not normally *hear* a person smoking. Of course, you can invent a referential world where there are horses that smoke and they smoke oranges and it makes a certain noise that you can hear; but, in the normal referential world, these are not acceptable arrangements of the concepts—i.e., they are inappropriately related.

Structural coherence can be further illustrated by the two statements: "He put his umbrella up" and "it started to rain." As separate statements, they are perfectly acceptable. You can also say "He put his umbrella up *because* it started to rain." That is an acceptable relationship between the two in the normal referential world. But other relationships can be posited which would not be acceptable, given those two original statements. For example, "He put his umbrella up, and *therefore* it started to rain." If you were one of those people who believe that every time they wash the car it rains, you might also believe that every time you put your umbrella up it starts to rain. In that case, this would be an acceptable sequence of thought, perhaps in the referential world of superstition, but not in the normal referential world. There is no cause-effect connection between putting your umbrella up and, as a consequence, it starting to rain. Still less could you say, "He put his umbrella up *although* it started to rain," because putting it up would be the expected thing to do if it started to rain. Least of all could you say, "He put his umbrella up; *that is to say*, it started to rain." "It started to rain" is clearly not a restatement of "He put his umbrella up." So you can have two perfectly acceptable statements, but there is only a limited number of relations that are appropriate for them when linked together.

Pursuing the distinction between referential coherence and structural coherence further, consider "A cigarette is smoking that man." This is an example of structural incoherence. Notice, however, that from the stand point of referential coherence, the concepts available—namely, cigarette, smokes, and man—are not incoherent. Referential coherence can be shown by correcting the structural incoherence so that the statement reads: "That man is smoking a cigarette." This gives both referential and structural coherence to the statement.

c. *Prominence.* The third analytical feature is that of prominence. This is the most neglected aspect of semantic structure, yet the basic idea had already been propounded by John Ruskin over a hundred years ago. In an essay on composition (Ruskin 1947:163–165) Ruskin discussed the "law of principality":

The great object of composition being always to secure unity; this is, to make out of many things one whole; the first mode in which this can be effected is, by determin-ing that one feature shall be more important than all the rest, and that the others shall group with it in subordinate positions

This is the simplest law of ordinary ornamentation. Thus the group of two leaves, a, Figure 1, is unsatisfactory, because it has no leading leaf; but that at b is prettier, be-cause it has a head or master leaf; and c more satisfactory still, because the subordina-tion of the other members to this head leaf is made more manifest by their gradual loss of size as they fall back from it...

a   b   c

Figure 1.

Thus, also, good pictures have always one light larger or brighter than the other lights, or one figure more prominent than the other figures, or one mass of colour dominant over all the other masses...This may be illustrated by musical melody; for in-stance in such phrases as this:

One note (here the upper G) rules the whole passage, and has the full energy of it concentrated in itself.

Prominence is simply making one or more parts of a unit more important than the other parts. Any well-formed discourse will do this. Otherwise, it just goes on monotonously and nothing is highlighted. The difference between a politician and a good teacher is probably along this line. The politician may not want to make any promise or pledge stand out, in order that he not be held accountable for it. So he may talk very fluently for half an hour without ever highlighting anything. You then go home and talk to someone else, and he asks, "Well, what did he say?" You reply, "Well, he spoke very fluently, and it was very impressive, and he really carried people with him." "But what did he actually say?" You cannot remember because nothing was made prominent. You find it very difficult to really pin anything down. Some sermons are like that, too. You get a very rosy impression, but you cannot actually remember what was said. That is usually because prominence features are either deliberately or inadvertently omitted so that the point was not put across. A good teacher, on the other hand, takes pains to make sure that the important points are made clear to his students; so he relies heavily on the features of prominence and the inventory of devices his particular language uses to manifest them.

Prominence must be considered from three interrelated perspectives: (a) the type of unit, i.e., concepts, propositions, or propositional configurations; (b) the kind of meaning, i.e., referential, situational, or structural; and (c) the kind of prominence, i.e., natural or marked.

When analyzing the prominence of a unit, it is quite important to keep hierarchical considerations in mind. That is, prominent information in a particular proposition or propositional cluster of a paragraph will not necessarily mean that that information will be among the most prominent information (the theme) of the paragraph. So also, what is prominent, or thematic, in a paragraph will not necessarily be thematic in the grouping of paragraphs (a section); and so on.

Prominence can be divided into natural and marked prominence. Every semantic unit of whatever type has *natural prominence,* what might be termed the organizational or relational center of the unit. Most often this refers to the central constituent of a semantic unit to which all the other constituents are directly or indirectly related; it is the hub of the wheel. *Marked prominence* is optional and does not therefore occur in every semantic unit. Any constituent within a unit may be marked as particularly significant. This does not replace the natural prominence but occurs in addition to it.

When a number of components are combined into a *concept,* the central (i.e., naturally prominent) component makes it possible for that concept to refer to a single segment of the referential world. The central component is the referential nucleus of the concept. However, in context, a non-nuclear component of a concept may be made focal (i.e., it may be given marked prominence). This will often be through the interplay of situational (e.g., connotative) and/or structural (e.g., collocational) information.

When a number of concepts are combined into a *proposition,* one of them will be the referential nucleus of the proposition, the others being directly or indirectly related to it. Furthermore, in a proposition, there is a structurally prominent part, which may be called the "comment." The "topic" of a proposition represents what is being spoken about or written about. The "comment" is that which is being said about the topic. In addition, any concept in a proposition may be given marked prominence, sometimes called special prominence or "focus."

A *propositional configuration* consists of two or more propositions, and where there are a number of propositions, there is a series of comments on one or more topics. This series of propositions would be a conglomerate mass if there were no prominence feature separating out one (or more) from the rest. But this is not what is found in language. There is a main topic which combines with the main comment, and this combination represents the *theme,* or at least the main part of the theme. The theme, then, consists mainly of the central constituent, that is to say, the main proposition, to which all the other propositions are related. As with the concept and the proposition, there may be marked prominence on a constituent other than the main one. This marked constituent, together with the main one, would then constitute the theme.

Subordination, a surface-structure phenomenon found in all languages, is a grammatical means by which to communicate different levels of thematicity. Those elements which are subordinated are of lesser rank, and just as there are levels of subordination, so, corresponding to that, there are levels of thematicity. We expect, therefore, that the grammar of a language, specifically the subordination patterns of a language, will point to the information which is of greatest thematic import in a given unit. While subordination is probably the chief device that indicates thematic rank, there are other devices which do this also. The finite form of the verb, for example, will more often carry greater thematic rank than those forms of the verb which are not finite. (It is necessary, however, to recognize that the use of nonfinite forms of the verb may be for other purposes, without indicating or having any implications concerning the level of thematicity of these units.)

2.3.2 The holistic features of semantic units

From figure 2.4, it can be seen that there are three holistic features of a semantic unit corresponding to the three analytical features which have been discussed. They are classification, external coherence, and thematic content. These arise from looking at a unit *as a whole*, rather than taking it apart and seeing how it is put together.

a. *Class*. When a semantic unit is taken as a whole, and the question is asked: What sort or class of information is this unit communicating?, then the answer to that question is its classification.

The smallest semantic unit is the concept, and it names or refers to segments of the referential world about which the author is communicating. The segments of that world can be grouped into four major categories: Things (T), Events (E), Attributes (A), and Relations (R). (These classes are discussed in detail later, section 5.3.1.) Likewise, concepts are grouped into four classes, according to the kind of segment of the referential world they refer to. Therefore, classified on the basis of the referential information conveyed, the concept may be a Thing, an Event, an Attribute, or a Relation.

It is also possible to classify a concept on the basis of the situational meaning that it conveys. Consider, for example, the words "dog" and "mutt." Each may be used to refer to the same specific animal in the same set of circumstances; thus, the referential content of the concept conveyed by both of these words is essentially the same (animal, canine, domesticated, etc.) with the same generic classification—a Thing. However, these two concepts differ quite radically in their situational content (in this case, the connotative content, which indicates the attitude of the author toward the referent). Classification of a concept on the basis of both the referential and situational content will often be quite essential to a translator as he seeks an equivalent expression in a receptor language.

At the next level of the hierarchy, i.e., the proposition, the information must also be classified in terms of both its referential and situational information—i.e., its central concept and its communication perspective. Classifying the proposition according to the central concept gives four types: state propositions and three kinds of event propositions (actions, processes, and experiences). At the same time, the proposition always assumes at least the following six situational elements: mood, time, aspect, polarity, tone, and register. Put the other way around, these six elements are inherent in a communication. One cannot communicate without assuming a communication situation indicated by mood, a time and/or aspect frame, either a negative or positive polarity, emotive overtones, and a social register.

As soon as mood is considered in an event or state proposition, it is then classifiable as belonging to one of the illocutionary classes: *statement*, *command*, or *question*. However, these are very generic classes since there are different kinds of each of them. A statement can be classified more specifically when some or all of the situational elements of time, aspect, polarity, tone, and register are considered. For example, a statement that is positive makes an "affirmation," one that is negative, a "denial." An affirmation that is future (or its equivalent aspect) will be, for example, a "promise," "threat," or "prediction."

In addition, there is the further factor of *tone*, i.e., emotive overtones such as displeasure, joy, anger, etc. Tone also includes such matters as degrees of authority, sincerity, and intensity. For example, the difference between "to beg" and "to demand" is one of degree of authority and indicates a different relationship between the speaker and the addressee. There is also *register*, i.e., the degree of formality with which the information is communicated. Both tone and register are closely related to the communication situation within which the discourse was composed.

A habitual aspect or tense form will give a "custom" or "general information."

> He came here every day at six.
> The sun always shines in California.

Past or present tense will give a "report," a "wish," a "desire," a "need," a "reminder," an "obligation," and others.

The sun was/is shining	report
He went to New York	report
I am not in New York	report
I do not want ice cream	desire
He should go	obligation

The first three examples are labeled "report," which is a rather generic term. More specific subclassifications of report would be:

accusation	explanation	obituary	argument
praise	illustration	consolation	excuse
ridicule	example	correction	description
exoneration	advertisement	orientation	enticement

The classification of a command or prohibition can be made more precise by noting tone. For example, there may be any of the following types:

a suggestion	a summons	a petition	a plan
an order	a challenge	an offer	a proposal
an invitation	a counsel	a regulation	a demand
advice	a direction	a claim	an admonition
a warning	a request	an instruction	a decree
a prohibition	a prayer	an obligation	

Long though these lists are, they are not considered to be complete.

The implication of this is that a proposition can be fully classified only by consideration of the situational context. The difficulty of doing that is greatly compounded when the discourse is written. If the context is not explicitly stated in a written communication, then there is no alternative but to select that which is most probable. The proposition "I have a headache" can be classed as an assertion without further context, but it could only be subclassed as a request or an apology by knowing the communication situation. For example, in a situation where there was quite a bit of noise, it would probably be a request for quiet. Or, in a situation with a close relationship between a mother and child, it would probably be understood as a request for medication.

This same assertion could be classified as an apology if it were made after a poor performance as an excuse or a reason for not having done well. On the other hand, it could be an apology or an excuse after one has been invited to participate in some games or other activity and would therefore be interpreted as a way in which to decline an invitation.

The next larger unit, the propositional cluster (the lowest-level subtype of propositional configurations), combines two or more propositions, with the result that it communicates a combination of actions, processes, experiences, or states, together with a combination of the situational, or communicational, aspects noted above for the proposition. The classification of the propositional cluster is, therefore, generally based on the same parameters as a single proposition.

There is not, however, complete identity of classification between the proposition and the cluster. In particular, there are some classifications that require a minimum of two propositions. In his article, "Assertions, Conditional Speech Acts, and Practical Inferences" (1977:13–46), D. Wunderlich discusses what he terms "negotiation" and "extortion." An example of the former would be "If you check my car brakes for me, I'll cook you one of your favorite pizzas." An example of the latter would be, "If you don't mow the front yard tonight, you won't get any supper." It is hard to conceive of either "negotiation" or "extortion" being classifications of a single proposition. Also, it could be argued that, while a prohibition can be a single proposition, e.g., "Keep out," "Do not touch," warnings and threats require at least two. Thus, "Danger: Keep out" would be a warning, because it states (very generically in this case) the grounds for the prohibition. Similarly, threats are commonly in the form of clusters: "Don't tease the dog, or you will get thrashed" or "If you tease the dog, you will get thrashed."

Moving further up the hierarchy, a paragraph makes use of propositions and propositional clusters to form a larger communication unit, one which develops a topic. The topic may be described, narrated, expounded, or, in the case of "how to" topics, the paragraph may give directions concerning a procedure to be followed. The paragraph may also function to exhort someone about a given course of action, or it may report a conversation related to some topic. Thus, for the paragraph (and also larger units, such as section or episode), there is a generic set of classifications in terms of what are called *discourse genres*— narration, exposition, procedure, exhortation, and dialogue.

As was the case with the proposition, so also the paragraph can be subclassified on the basis of situational aspects of meaning. Consider, for example, the specific subclassifications listed above in this section. These are applicable (with some exceptions, doubtless) to all communication units, regardless of complexity and level in the hierarchy. Take, for instance, the various subclassifications of "report" (listed above)—accusation, praise, ridicule, exoneration, etc. These could equally well be classifications of a paragraph or higher-level units.

The narrative genre, a highly generic classification, may be further classified by subgenres, such as historical narrative, epic narrative, fiction, biography, etc. Then these subgenres may be further subclassified on the basis of situational considerations as above.

b. *External coherence.* The second holistic feature of a semantic unit, external coherence, is a corollary to the principles of hierarchy and internal coherence. That is to say, a semantic unit will not only have constituents that are compatible with one another and appropriately related to one another, but it will also itself be a constituent of a higher-level semantic unit and must be compatible with the other constituents of that higher-level unit and appropriately related to them. Viewed, then, in terms of its distribution, a semantic unit is expected to be both referentially and situationally compatible with the other units to which it is related. Furthermore, it will be playing a specifiable role in the relational structure of the unit of which it is a part.

More needs to be said concerning the role of a unit as a corollary of the relations between it and other units. Relations have a double function. They tie together parts to form a whole and, in so doing, they are an essential feature of the internal coherence of the unit. In the process of doing so, however, they also indicate a certain role for each constituent. That is to say, they indicate what role the constituent is playing in the development of the unit it is a part of. It follows from this that the role of a semantic unit can only be known when that unit is seen in context. Thus, the concept "boy" has no role meaning until it is placed in context. As soon as it is, it will assume a role such as Agent, Affectant, Beneficiary, etc. Propositions also take on a role in context. The relational system not only indicates connections among communication units (propositions and propositional configurations), but along with the information content, it also indicates a particular role for each communication unit, such as reason, condition, etc. Because of this, we can speak of a reason proposition or a condition proposition, etc. From the point of view of role, therefore, a communication unit may serve as the head of a larger communication unit or as a clarificational, orientational, logical, or stimulus-response constituent of it. Communication units can also serve to describe, identify, or comment on a concept. (See chapter 8 for a full discussion of the system of communication relations.)

c. *Thematic content.* The third holistic feature answers the question, "What is the unit about?" or "What prominent information does the unit convey?" The answer to these questions will be the thematic content of the unit.

A significant consideration of the thematic content of a unit is the situational aspect of *purpose.* Earlier in this paper, in the discussion of the communication situation, it was stated that there was some specific aspect of the situation that stimulated the author to compose his particular discourse. In light of this specific situation, the author has an overall purpose in mind. However, this purpose may or may not be stated explicitly. In the case of the New Testament books, for instance, an explicit purpose is sometimes given. In the Gospel of John the following explicit purpose is revealed: "These things are written that you may believe that Jesus is the Christ, the Son of God, and that believing you may have life in his name" (20:31).

Even if the purpose is not stated explicitly, the other thematic material at the higher levels will implicitly indicate the author's purpose. For example, a possible theme statement for the entire book of Acts would be "The word of the Lord has been believed in various locations in spite of much opposition." Luke's purpose, then, in writing the book of Acts seems to be to bolster the Christians' belief in the gospel and to persuade nonbelievers to become Christians. He attempted to do this by showing the credibility of the gospel, by describing how it had spread to many localities and had been believed there in spite of considerable opposition.

So far, we have spoken only of an "overall" purpose that an author has in producing a discourse. (It should be noted, in passing, that an author's overall purpose may simply be to entertain, or to amuse, as would be the case with many novels.) But every communication unit is considered to have a purpose, i.e., no information is expressed in a discourse without some purpose. Experience indicates, however, that clearly stable purposes seem normally to be discernible from the section level upwards. A particular paragraph may have a discernible purpose, but it is more commonly the case that purpose becomes discrete and stable when paragraphs are combined into sections. The purpose of units below such levels appear to simply contribute to the higher-level purpose.

A good example of section and paragraph purposes is provided by 1 Cor. 10:1–22. These verses constitute a section, consisting of a number of paragraphs, and the theme of the section is stated in 10:14: "Flee from idolatry" (NIV). Hence, the purpose is to warn the Corinthians about the danger of idolatry. The first paragraph in this section is 10:1–5, and its purpose is to remind (less likely, inform) the Corinthians of the experiences of the Israelites at the time of the exodus. These historical facts provide (illustrative) grounds for what Paul goes on to say. So, although the purpose of the first paragraph, verses 1–5, is not that of warning, its own purpose of reminding plays an integral part in the overall purpose of the section.

It is useful to recognize that often there is both a more immediate purpose and a more distant one, the one leading to the other. The purpose of John's Gospel, quoted on the previous page, appears to be of this sort. The immediate purpose is that the reader might believe that Jesus is the Christ, the Son of God; the further purpose is that the reader might have (eternal) life.

It is also possible for an author to have a covert purpose, that is, one that is contrary to, or distinctly different from, the purpose that the overt content would indicate. For example, the apparent purpose of certain types of fraudulent advertisement is to offer a person some useful and worthwhile service. But the covert purpose is to deceive him and obtain money from him. A questionnaire may have the overt purpose of obtaining information for statistical purposes, but the covert purpose may be that of obtaining specimens of your handwriting for the further covert purpose of forgery. In the nature of the case, such covert purposes cannot be deduced from the overt content of the discourse, but can only be known from situational information, external to the discourse in question.

The classification of a unit is closely related to its theme and purpose. Thus, to use the example from Acts, these features of the total book can be related as follows: "I have narrated (to you) that the word of the Lord has been believed in various locations in spite of much opposition in order that you may know that the word of the Lord is to be believed." "I have narrated (to you)" is derived from the genre classification (i.e., narrative); it is followed by the central thematic content; and this leads, in turn, to the purpose. Put somewhat differently, the means chosen by Luke, with his particular purpose in mind, was a narrative (specifically, an historical account) with that particular main theme. This is true at lower levels also. A particular class of unit is the means chosen to convey the main thematic content in order to achieve the purpose.

Nothing has been said so far about the purpose of a concept. A concept is not a communication unit (proposition or configuration), but a referring one. That is to say, its purpose is to name or circumscribe discrete segments of the world the author wishes to speak about; specifically, the concept refers to Things, Events, Attributes, and Relations discerned and distinguished in that world. If the author wishes to speak of worlds outside those handled by his language, then he has to invent new words or expressions with which to refer to this new world something which scientists (with positrons and quasars), linguists (with morphemes and archiphoneme), and novelists (with hobbits and orcs) are constantly doing.

2.4 The Particle, Wave, and Field Perspective

Anyone familiar with Kenneth Pike's emphasis on particle, wave, and field in linguistics (1959) is bound to be struck by the appearance of "threesomes" in semantic structure. The feature of constituency (unity) can readily be compared with the notion of particle; coherence, with that of field; and prominence, with that of wave. All three are essential to account for all the facets of semantic structure.

3

THE RELATIONSHIP OF SEMANTIC STRUCTURE
TO SURFACE STRUCTURE

3.1 The Three Analytical Features are Universals

An overview of the meaning features which are basic to semantic structure has been presented. The analytical features of constituency, coherence, and prominence may be properly considered a universal, applicable to any entity. As has been pointed out, these represent a triad which is evident in both physical and psychological reality. It is something that the human both recognizes and/or imposes on anything that is divisible into parts. We have noted that in modes of expression other than language, such as music or art, these three features are significant. It is very likely that they are inherent categories of the mind, and as such, must be reckoned with as factors which predetermine what a normal mind will produce.

3.2 There are Three Hierarchies in Language

There are three simultaneously occurring hierarchies assumed in the theory of language presented here. They are the phonological, grammatical, and semantic hierarchies. The first deals with sounds and their arrangements; the second with grammatical units and their formal arrangements; and the third with information and its arrangement into semantic units.

To summarize what this means, we may more simply say: sounds are used to form grammatical units which, in turn, "encode," "represent," or "realize" ideas. Stating this in the reverse: ideas of the mind are represented by words arranged properly into grammatical units, which, in turn, are expressed physically, primarily by vocal sounds and secondarily by writing. This, of course, is an over-simplification of the interrelationship of the three hierarchies. Nevertheless, it serves to indicate the general relationship between them.

3.3 The Semantic Hierarchy is the "Master" Hierarchy

The semantic hierarchy may be dubbed the "master" hierarchy with the other two as its "servants." The phonological and grammatical hierarchies serve as vehicles to give a formal representation to meaning—the semantic hierarchy. This can be diagrammed as follows:

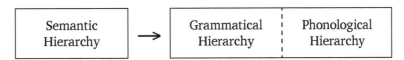

Without these "servants," however, we would be at a loss to know where to start or how to analyze the semantic hierarchy. The function of the phonological hierarchy is primarily to provide perceptible substance to meaning by means of sounds, so as to distinguish words from one another. In addition, however, the phonological system communicates meaning through phenomena such as stress and intonation patterns. These can communicate, among other things, attitudes such as anger, pleading, jocularity, etc. These phonological signals are for the most part not present in written material, but the meaning they are intended to convey can be recovered by expressing it explicitly in such ways as "he spoke *angrily*," "she said *with a pleading tone of voice*," etc. Perhaps it can also be recovered, at least in part, by punctuation. Alliteration and rhyme are phonological devices which often serve for aesthetic purposes or to mark prominence. For example, alliteration is frequently used to highlight or give emphasis to selected ideas.

The phonological and grammatical hierarchies together constitute the surface structure of a language, which represents the form component of the form-meaning composite that is fundamental to communication. If information proceeds from and is formulated in the mind, it follows that the surface structure form which is chosen to encode the ideas of the mind is, on the one hand, distinct from and subservient to the conceptual process and, on the other hand, is absolutely essential if one wishes to communicate those conceptual notions.

Although the semantic and grammatical hierarchies are distinct and differ in many respects, it is nonetheless the case that the nuclei of grammatical construction types closely coincide with the central constituents found in semantic structure; that is to say, they coincide quite closely with the analytical feature of prominence.

It is possible to think of communication as giving rise to or implying groupings of information which are then expressed by grammatical units. Similarly, coherence implies relations and roles which are then manifested by relations in the grammatical hierarchy of the language. Thirdly, prominence implies thematic content and purpose in the semantic structure which then manifests itself by the grammatical hierarchy in the superordinate and nuclear part of whatever unit is under analysis.

The movement from cognitive notions to speech (or writing) is known as the "encoding" process. The "decoding" process is the reverse—movement from speech or writing to cognitive notions. This is the process that is involved in analyzing the surface forms of any written communication (including the Bible) and deriving from them an understanding of what the writers were attempting to communicate to their readers. This overview has focused primarily on the encoding process as a means to better understand the decoding process.

3.4 Skewing Between the Semantic and Grammatical Hierarchies

The emphasis on the encoding process throughout this overview may have given the impression that there is a direct and simple one-to-one representation of the semantic structure in the grammatical hierarchy, but this is far from being the case. Both direct matching and skewing (mismatching) occur commonly in all languages. Skewing occurs in a variety of ways. For example, the *units* of the semantic hierarchy may or may not match those used in the grammatical hierarchy; the semantic and grammatical *classes* are often different; the semantic *relations/roles* may be signaled by a variety of lexical forms and/or grammatical constructions. Chapters 14–16 in *Translating the Word of God* (Beekman and Callow 1974) are devoted entirely to a discussion of skewing between meaning and its formal representation in Koiné Greek. (See also, for example, Langendoen 1970:156–157, and Wunderlich 1977 for discussions of this phenomenon in English.)

Figure 3.1 attempts to display both matching and skewing. The solid lines represent a matched representation of the semantic structure; the broken lines a skewed representation. Skewing and matching are shown in three areas: units, classification, and some relations/roles.

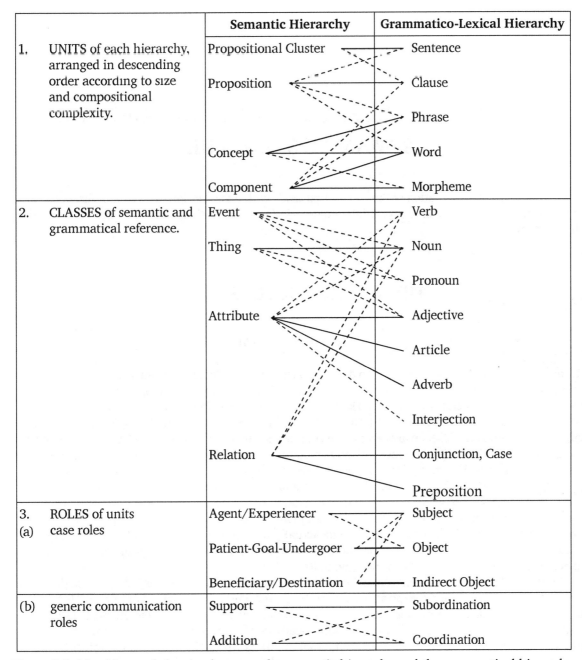

Figure 3.1. Matching and skewing between the semantic hierarchy and the grammatical hierarchy.

PART II
A DETAILED PRESENTATION OF THE THEORY OF SEMANTIC STRUCTURE

This more detailed presentation of the theory first deals with a description of the major discourse types (chapter 4), and then goes on to give a detailed description of the various semantic units introduced in the overview.

4
THE MAJOR DISCOURSE TYPES

4.0 Introduction

In the overview, it was explained that an author's purpose generally arises from some specific situation within the total communication situation. This purpose leads him to select a topic from all possible topics about which he intends to comment. He determines what he wishes to communicate about that topic, which involves a selection on his part from all that could be said concerning the topic, given his knowledge of it. At the same time, he arranges these comments into an organized and structured framework to accomplish his purpose in the most effective manner, given his level of competence in the use of his linguistic resources. This gives rise to different discourse types.

It must be granted from the start, however, that any division of literature into discourse or literary types represents an abstraction from actual discourse, in which dominant patterns are recognized which provide the basis for the distinctions made. It should not be expected, however, that pure discourse types will be typical. To the contrary, what one actually finds is a combination of two or more types within a particular communication. For example, narration may contain description and exposition; or exposition may contain narrative or dialogue units.

Perhaps the above statements could be formulated more precisely. What is being said is that a discourse is classed as narration, exposition, exhortation, procedure, or dialogue on the grounds that larger units which provide the framework of the discourse are narrative, expository, etc. In most cases, this will probably mean that such units are also numerically dominant. But individual paragraphs and larger units can be, and often are, of a different type from the framework. Thus, the Gospels might be classed as a special type of exposition, since the principle underlying their organization is not so much the chronology of the matters dealt with, but rather the thesis of the author, the point he is trying to make. In spite of their broad classification as exposition, they are widely regarded as narration, since the vast majority of the material contained in them is narration. They also contain long passages of teaching, such as the Sermon on the Mount (three chapters in length), which would be classed as exposition. Similarly, Paul's epistles would be regarded as exhortation, yet there is a clear division in a number of them between the opening expository material, and the subsequent hortatory material. And an Old Testament book such as Exodus contains extensive examples of narration, exposition, exhortation, and procedure. In spite of the relative lack of uniform examples, however, it is still useful, for analytical purposes, to classify a total discourse according to its predominant pattern.

4.1 Conversation and Discourse Genre

Before discussing the characteristic features of the major discourse types in more detail, it is necessary to relate these types to *conversation*. It seems a reasonable assumption that conversation is the basic form of human communication—speaker A talking to participant B and B replying; or A, B, and C talking together; etc. And as the basic form, it readily makes use of all of the major types—a speaker may tell a story, argue a point, give instructions regarding how something is to be done, urge conduct on others. Conversation, then, is viewed as a "situational framework" within which the major types are found. *Monologue* is simply a special form of conversation in which only one person does the speaking or writing. And, just like conversation, monologue can, and does, make use of all types of discourse. Note, however, that monologue, particularly narrative monologue, can report a conversation; so that, in this sort of "embedding," a conversation becomes a particular form of monologue. For convenience in distinguishing the situational conversations from referential ones, the label *dialogue* is used to refer to the latter. Dialogue may take the form of speech within the framework of one of the other major discourse types—usually narrative—or it may so extensively characterize the discourse as to constitute a separate genre, or at least subgenre (e.g., plays).

4.2 The Major Discourse Types Defined

4.2.1 Expository discourse

Expository discourse typically answers such questions as: "What is claimed and why?" "What is the explanation of X?" "Why is X so?" It embraces all discourse that has as its purpose definition, explanation, information, or interpretation. It is probably one of the most frequently used forms of discourse, for it includes most technical and scientific material, most textbooks, the majority of magazine articles, essays, editorials, and reviews. By and large, expository discourse consists of logically related sequences of propositions, with such relations as generic-specific, reason-result, and grounds-conclusion occurring frequently.

4.2.2 Hortatory discourse

In hortatory discourse, the author prescribes a course of action, which he supports with grounds to justify such a request or proposal and to motivate the addressee(s) to act upon the request, proposal, or command. The purpose is thus eminently practical, i.e., the author seeks to persuade his addressee(s) to accept his views and to act upon his suggestions or directives. Hortatory discourse typically answers the questions: "What should be done?" and "Why should it be done?"

Hortatory discourse, for the most part, consists of logically related sequences of propositions with the grounds-exhortation relation dominant. It must be understood that it is only in extreme cases that hortatory discourse frees itself completely from exposition, so that the line which separates hortatory discourse from expository discourse is not always clear. However, a fairly consistent classification can be made on the following basis. If the head of a unit (of any level) is a command, that unit is hortatory, regardless of how much exposition it contains, and regardless of whether it may be a part of an expository unit; and if the head of a unit is a statement, that unit is not hortatory, even though it may contain hortatory constituents and may itself be a part of a larger hortatory unit.

4.2.3 Procedural discourse

The question which typifies procedural discourse is: "How is X done?" Procedural discourse thus consists primarily of chronologically based sequences of actions with either command, means-result, or means-purpose functions dominant. Notice, therefore, that time, or, more strictly speaking, succession in time, is significant to the structure. Logical relations indeed are present, but clearly within a basic time framework. This is not true of expository and hortatory discourse, in which there is no basic time framework. Rather, in these two types of discourse, both the framework and the dominating relations are logical.

4.2.4 Narrative discourse

The typical question asked (or answered) by narration is: "What happened?" and "How did it happen?" Of course, the reader also wants to know: "Who did it and where and when was it done?" so that answers to these questions become essential elements in most narratives. Narration, therefore, is generally introduced with a setting and then focuses on incidents involving specified participants. They consist primarily of a sequential chronological framework of events, in which the stimulus-response relations are dominant.

a. *Narration without plot.* There are two types of narration: narration without plot and narration with plot. Narration without plot is a simple chronological sequence of propositions related, in its minimal form, only by addition. An example would be an account of one's activities throughout a given time period, covering a number of different locations visited and some brief activity accomplished at each place. Children's early efforts at writing essays are often of this type: "I went home and I ate my supper and then I played with my dog. Then I went outside and went to my friend June's house and we played together and..."

b. *Narration with plot.* The second type of narration is that which has plot structure. Within this broad classification, two kinds of plot structure can be usefully distinguished—plots that involve some struggle or contest, and those that do not. Put another way, narrative episodes, scenes, acts, etc., that do not involve the stimulus role of *problem* are "nonproblem" narratives, those that do involve it are "problem" narratives.

Nonproblem narratives are built around a pair of stimulus-response roles such as occasion-outcome, remark-evaluation, and question-answer. While many of the episodes and larger units in the Gospels and Acts are examples of problem-based narratives, there are also examples of nonproblem narratives (see, for example, Mark 1:16–18 and 19–20).

In a problem-based narrative, the struggle may be very elemental and physical—animal against animal, animal against environment, man against nature, man against man, man against animal. The conflict may be between man and society, conventions, or business conditions. Sometimes the conflict is a moral struggle. The conflict gives rise to those actions and interactions that move toward a resolution of the conflict. In the process, there will often be a heightening of the conflict which reaches a peak or climax just before or at the point where the resolution takes place.

4.3 Parameters of the Major Discourse Types

The major discourse types may be distinguished by two sets of parameters. (For another approach to distinguishing major discourse types, see Longacre 1980:19–23.) The first set is the presence or absence of a chronological framework within which the logical relations are presented. The second set is the presence or absence of the prescription, often in the form of command. All types of discourse use logical relations, since they are all examples of rational discourse, but in narrative and procedural discourse there is a chronological framework—events in a narration and steps in a procedure are presented as necessarily chronologically successive. Figure 4.1 displays these features.

	NONPRESCRIPTIVE	**PRESCRIPTIVE**
Logical relations presented within a chronological framework	Narrative Discourse	Procedural Discourse
Logical relations presented without a chronological framework	Expository Discourse	Hortatory Discourse

Figure 4.1. Parameters distinguishing the major discourse types.

The expression "time-line" is used in connection with the chronological framework. It is essentially the same as what Longacre (1980:34ff) calls "mainline" or more specifically "event-line." Others have used the terms "foreground" and "backbone" to speak of this notion. Much discourse analysis has been concerned with narration, and in this context, time-line has become a widely accepted concept. It refers to the main sequence of events around which a narrative is built—i.e., events which follow one another in time. By this definition, many events will be excluded from the time-line. Those which provide explanations, or give reasons, or describe or identify participants are thereby excluded from the time-line. Several simultaneous events would be allotted one place on the time-line.

Indeed, much emphasis has been put on the significance of the chronological framework in distinguishing discourse types. However, as figure 4.1 indicates, the characteristic feature of rational discourse, including narrative, is that it uses "logical relations." So while the fact of a time-line is readily acknowledged, it is considered to be subservient to the logical relations which make clear what function in the total structure of the narrative the time-line events have.

It should be mentioned at this point that some rhetoricians establish another major discourse genre called "description." The question which description typically answers is: "What is X like?" Herein, it is considered to be a minor discourse type which consists of logically related sequences of propositions describing a Thing or Attribute. Description is most likely to be found in connection with narration and exposition. It plays a secondary function in a story or explanation. Descriptions usually appeal to any of the five senses, describing what is seen, heard, tasted, touched, or smelled.

4.4 Discourse Types and the Author's Purpose

There are four major genre types which have been mentioned, namely, exposition, exhortation, procedure, and narration. The first three parallel three author purposes: to explain or argue for a thesis, to urge a course of action, and to tell how something is done. These "nonnarrative" types give a good estimate of the author's purpose, since the genre and the purpose are closely tied together.

Narrative genre is different in this respect. Its overt purpose would seem to be "to recount," but the question can always be asked *Why* recount this? The answer to that question is likely to be much nearer the author's purpose. In Galatians, for example, Paul gives a narrative account of some of his significant early experiences as a Christian (see 1:13–2:21), but the purpose is stated to be to vindicate his claim that his gospel was not man-made. Again, with each of the Gospels, we have a narrative discourse, but what was the purpose of the authors? Was it simply to recount events in the life of Christ? No, it would be generally agreed that for each Gospel as a whole it was to portray Jesus as Israel's Messiah-King, or as the Son of God, or the Messiah-Prophet, etc., almost certainly with the further purpose to confirm or produce faith in Jesus. For collections of episodes or for individual episodes contained in a Gospel, it is possible to identify the purpose the author is aiming to achieve.

From the above discussion, it can be seen that, if one knows the major genre of a nonnarrative composition, by virtue of that classification he receives a clue as to the author's purpose. For, whenever an author chooses a purpose and decides which arrangement of the material will accomplish that purpose most effectively, he places himself under certain structural constraints within which he will compose his communication; he then moves into a choice of more specific genres and subgenres. With narrative genre, however, the classification as narration tells the investigator relatively less; the overall theme of the narrative needs to be known before it is possible to begin to arrive at the author's purpose when using the narrative genre. (This will be discussed more fully in chapter 10.)

4.5 Discourse Types and Specific Genres

The major discourse types have been noted and briefly described, but little has been said of any subtypes, i.e., specific genres. The specific genres of some discourses are derived from the kind of main character in focus—for example, a hero in epic, a shepherd in pastoral, and a historical figure in biography. On the other hand, they may be derived from the topic or from the psychological mood. Thus, specific genre types may be as numerous as there are distinct subjects about which one may speak or write or attitudes which may be expressed (such as satire). The following is a partial listing of specific genre types: biography, diary, fiction, folklore, newspaper reports, myth, novel, short story, anecdote, proverb, tale, joke, riddle, legend, obituary, eulogy, prayer, service manual, how-to, history, recipes. However, it is recognized that these classifications need further refining, as some are still very generic (fiction, tale, history) while others are more specific (obituary, eulogy, joke). Also, some would be relevant to greater lengths of discourse (novel, history, how-to), while others would be relevant to discourses with much shorter lengths (short story, anecdote, proverb, riddle, recipe.) Thus, a "short story" could include within it several anecdotes, a joke, and an obituary, eulogy, or prayer. Further, some of these classifications could be of considerably different lengths (or degree of development), such as a newspaper report (half a column to a 2-page spread), a legend (short story length to book size), or prayer (a paragraph to several sections). There is also the question of how such distinctions as poetry versus prose are to be related to the four genres.

5

THE CONCEPT

5.0 Introduction

The concept may be defined as "a cognitive construct that refers to or correlates with a segment of the individual 'world'." By saying that the concept is a "cognitive" entity, we intend to point out that the concept is not a segment of the world itself, but rather is a product of a human being's conceptual ordering of it. By using the word "construct" we mean to emphasize that the particular segmentation and organization of that world is unique to the individual observer; that is, it is his unique segmentation and organization of "reality." By "world" is meant not only the perceptual or experiential world of the individual, but also imaginary worlds. That is to say, it encompasses any world that the individual may wish to think about or talk about. Since our focus in this work is upon communication, we will hereafter refer to this notion as the "referential realm"—i.e., the world to which the communicator wishes to refer.

Up to this point, we have spoken of the concept as a cognitive construct of an individual. Ultimately, it is true that concepts are unique to every individual. However, there is a very real sense in which a concept becomes the construct of a speech community. This is due to the tendency of aggregates of human beings who experience virtually the same physical and social environment and who engage in frequent and sustained interaction to develop a high degree of similarity and overlap in their conceptualization of their world. The result of this is that the concepts of the members of a speech community will for the most part be identical. Were this not so, communication would be virtually impossible.

With this brief introduction to the notion of the concept, we may now proceed to discuss the place of the concept in communication.

5.1 Lexical Versus Discourse Concepts

As was pointed out in chapter 2 (2.1.1), a speech community will "lexicalize," or assign a "name" to some of the concepts, while the vast majority of concepts are not so treated. Many of the concepts that are lexicalized are ones which are relatively generic and which are basic to the interests of the community. Most other lexicalized concepts are those which are commonly used by the speech community. These can then be clustered to express the other, almost infinite variety of more specific concepts about which the community wishes to talk.

From this it is clear that the term "concept" is used for two closely related, yet different, notions—i.e., lexical concepts and discourse concepts. The former has to do with the meaning (or set of meanings) underlying each of the lexical items of a particular language; the latter pertains to the constituents of the propositions of a specific discourse. These two kinds of concepts are closely associated in the sense that all lexical concepts are *potential* discourse concepts. The author of a discourse is restricted to the inventory of lexical concepts (i.e., the lexicon) as the building blocks for the more specific concepts he wishes to express in his discourse.

Discourse concepts differ from lexical concepts in two significant ways. First, they are no longer potential but actual expressed concepts. That is, they have a specific correlate in the referential realm of the discourse, whereas the lexical concept has an open-ended array of possible referents. Secondly, most discourse concepts are formed by combining two or more lexical concepts—e.g., the lexical concepts represented by the words "the," "big," "black," and "bear" combine to form the single discourse concept "the big black bear."

In spite of the differences, the two types of concept are analytically alike. That is, each is composed of a central generic component to which the other components relate by delimiting (i.e., making more specific) the generic component. Furthermore, there is a similarity in function. Both the lexical concept and the discourse concept serve to identify (circumscribe) a particular segment of the referential realm.

Our main concern is with discourse concepts; therefore, unless specifically stated, the word "concept" will be referring to the constituents of propositions.

5.2 The Concept Viewed Analytically

5.2.1 The constituents of the concept

Just as there are features such as voicing and closure which combine to form the first and smallest unit of the phonological hierarchy, the phoneme, so also in the semantic hierarchy there are components of meaning which combine to form the first and smallest unit, the concept. The concept may be said to consist of a combination of components of meaning, compatible with one another, appropriately related to one another, and one of which is central. The concept, with its componential versatility, makes it possible to refer to any segment of the particular world that the author wishes to talk about. Furthermore, it is possible to refer to totally new concepts, whether imaginary or foreign, simply by combining components in new ways.

It follows from the above description of the concept that it can be analyzed into components (features) of meaning. This is done by contrasting the concept (whether lexical or discourse) with other members of a generic class of concepts to which both it and they belong. This has been exemplified in detail for the verb "to run" in *Translating Word of God* (Beekman and Callow 1974:80–86). The components of its primary sense are shown to be the following:

1. To move oneself from one place to another (of animate beings with legs)
2. Repeated alternate use of both legs
3. Both feet leave the ground during the cycle
4. Progress is forward (unless specified differently)
5. Rate is rapid
6. Motion is on a solid surface

Of these six components, the first is the generic, central component. Each of the others is related to this central component by the general relation of *delimitation*; that is to say, they "narrow down" the very generic central component until the combination of components yields the particular concept the author wishes to use. In this case, components 2 through 5 describe the manner of moving oneself from one place to another (if one is an animate being with legs); component 6 describes the location of the movement.

Similarly, the concept "boy" can be analyzed into three components: human being (the central component), male, and young.

It is much more difficult to separate out the components of a concept like "hot," since it is a quality that has to do with relative points on a continuum. Thus "hot" is one concept used in connection with a temperature scale, together with such other concepts as "cold" and "lukewarm"; it represents the higher end of that relative scale. "Hot," then, has the generic component of "value on a temperature scale," the specific component being "greater than lukewarm or cold."

A lexical item like "since" is also difficult to analyze. It has two senses, each of which is regarded as a concept. One of the concepts has to do with time, and the other with cause and effect. This latter sense of "since" can be analyzed as having the following components:

1. A relation between two communication units (the central component)
2. Logical
3. Reason or grounds

A concept not only has a referential aspect—that which correlates with a specific segment of the referential world; it also has a situational aspect, commonly called "connotation"—that which correlates with the author's attitudes and values. Connotation can be considered as operating along at least two parameters: a *value* parameter and a *potency* parameter. The positive and negative poles of the value parameter are seen in such pairs as good/bad, beautiful/ugly, useful/useless, hero/villain. Examples of the poles of the potency parameter are strong/weak, success/failure, and clever/stupid. Many words, however, are connotationally neutral. In the context of a given discourse, the author will choose those concepts which carry the appropriate connotation for the overall tone of the discourse, or, if the tone varies, of a particular unit in the discourse.

5.2.2 The internal coherence of the concept

For a group of components to be regarded as a concept, it must exhibit internal coherence. There are two types of coherence within a concept: referential coherence and structural coherence.

Referential coherence requires that the components which are combined in the concept be semantically compatible. We normally expect to find qualities of motion (e.g., quickly, slowly, etc.) combined with Event notions (e.g., walk, work, etc.), not with Thing notions (e.g., house, dog, tree, etc.). Each of the parts of a concept must be experientially compatible with the rest, i.e., the total combination must be cognitively acceptable, must reflect the world to which the author wants to refer.

The *structural coherence* of the concept is shown by the components being appropriately related to the central component. All of the components are related to the central one either directly, or, in complex concepts (see below, section 5.3.1), indirectly, i.e., via another component. When further components are added to an Event concept, as in "ran quickly," "ate slowly," "glided effortlessly," etc., the added components "quickly," "slowly," and "effortlessly" relate to the Event concept as manner qualities. Generally, the manner component is descriptive, that is to say, it simply gives further information about the main part of the concept. However, it appears to be the case that, when a manner component is added to an Event which is in the imperative mood, i.e., a commanded Event, it is identificational, it picks this Event out as compared with others. This may be restricted to cases in which there is prominence on the manner component. Thus, in Col. 4:5, the Greek reads *en sophia peripateite* 'in wisdom be-walking', i.e., "walk wisely." The commanded action is "walk" and the manner component is "wisely." However, in the surface structure, the phrase *en sophia* 'in wisdom', which represents "wisely," is given marked prominence by being put before the verb. It has an identificational role, specifying the particular type of "walking" Paul is commanding, in contrast with other possible types. (Note that, in English, this can be shown by skewing, as in "Be wise in your conduct (= walk)" with the Attribute represented by a verb, the Event by a noun.)

It also seems likely that, in certain cases, an Attribute concept with prominence is best considered not to be a further component added to some Thing, but, in the semantic structure, a State proposition related to the whole proposition by one of the communication relations described in chapter 8. Consider, for example the statement:

An animal *that big* will never get through *there*!

In a semantic analysis, this could well be expressed as:

An animal as big as that is will never get through there, *because he is too big to do so.*

The extra proposition states the reason why "that big" is emphasized, and is therefore carried implicitly by the prominence marking.

5.2.3 Prominence within the concept

In the Overview (section 2.3.1 and figure 2.4), it was pointed out that prominence is an analytical feature of all units, and that a distinction can be drawn between natural and marked prominence. Natural prominence is signaled by the unmarked, or "normal," patterns of surface structure; marked prominence requires some special surface-structure device to indicate it. In the case of the concept, the naturally prominent component is the central one. This is the case because all the other components relate to it directly or indirectly; it is the relational center, the hub of the wheel. It can thus be determined apart from context by studying the internal structure of a concept.

Marked prominence in the concept has the effect of *highlighting* one or more of its components (usually a component other than the central one). Three approaches have been identified for achieving this highlighting: all-inclusive focus, contrastive focus, and intensive focus.

All-inclusive focus is given to a concept when its content is repeated by itemizing in some way or other. Thus, in *"All the people—old and young, men and women, adults and children—*fled to the safety of higher land," the concept "all the people" is given all-inclusive focus by the series of phrases which follows it, spelling out the details of "all the people." By doing so, the component of universality (i.e., "all") is highlighted.

Contrastive focus is given to a component of a concept when it is compared or contrasted with other possible like components by some means. Often this is done by phonological devices in English. It occurs on the component "blue" in, "No, I want *the BLUE pitcher!*" The italicized portion of this sentence represents a concept in which "pitcher" is the central constituent and therefore, the naturally prominent component. But the component "blue" is highlighted by being contrasted with nonblue qualities through the phonological devices of strong stress and a sharp pitch fall. In written communication, the same could be achieved using the cleft form "It is the *blue* pitcher that I want."

Intensive focus is given to a concept when an Attribute of degree is assigned to it by special surface-structure devices, such as the figure of speech called litotes. Paul's statement to the commander (Acts 21:39) that he was "a citizen of *no ordinary city*" (NIV) meant that he was a member of "a very important city," the litotes intensifying the Attribute "important." Another surface device used to represent intensive focus, one which is widespread in languages, is that of repetition. Consider, for example, Matt. 11:25, "You have hidden these things from *the wise and learned,*" where "wise and learned" is a repetition to intensify the notion of intellectual aptitude. Note also that the naturally prominent central component "human beings" is downplayed by its null representation in the surface structure. This adds to the highlighting of the noncentral component.

It should be noted that, generally speaking, in most languages there will be a variety of ways of highlighting components of a concept. For example, contrastive focus can also be shown by adding a negation: "I want the blue pitcher, not the red one." Intensive focus can be heightened by repeating the intensifying word, as in "He moved along the path *very, very slowly.*" In some languages the form that represents the particular component is itself repeated, as in "We've planned *a big, big show* for you." In New Testament Greek and many other languages, highlighting can be shown by special word orders.

Note, however, what happens when a concept is used with a figurative sense. For example, in the statement, "the kettle is boiling," "kettle" is used with the sense of "water." "Kettle" belongs to the generic class of kitchen utensils, along with bowl, pitcher, pot, pan, basin, etc., and would probably be distinguished from the other members of this class by its function. Its central constituent is therefore "container," and one of its specific components of meaning would be "used for boiling water." When it is used figuratively, as in the present example, the component "water," which is associated with a specifying component of the concept "kettle," occurs with marked prominence, and all the other components are, for all intents and purposes, canceled out by the figure (in this case, a metonymy).

The use of "pig" to convey the meaning of "greedy" is similar. "Greedy" is a component of meaning associated with "pig." When "pig" is used figuratively, all of the noncentral components except "greedy" are virtually canceled, and so also is the central constituent "animal," which is replaced with the component carrying marked focus.

Consider also the combination of concepts found in Rom. 12:1, "a living sacrifice." Here the use of the concept "living," used as a specifying component of the overall concept, cancels out one of the significant components associated with "sacrifice," namely, that the sacrifice is "killed." The remaining components continue in force in the context.

5.3 The Concept Viewed Holistically

5.3.1 The classification of the concept

a. *Referential classification.* All concepts, in whatever language, can be assigned to one of four universal classes: Things, Events, Attributes, and Relations (TEAR). This is done on the basis of the class of the central component of the concept. The class of Things includes all animate beings, natural and supernatural, and also all inanimate entities; that of Events includes all actions, processes (changes of state), and experiences; that of Attributes includes all features of quality and quantity that are ascribed to other concepts; that of Relations includes all relations that occur between any two semantic units.

T - boy, ghost, angel, stone, galaxy, blood, unicorn
E - to eat, to run, to think, to melt, to stretch, to smile, to hear
A - long, thick, soft, hot, slowly, suddenly, very few, six, all
R - with, by, because, since, then

In all of the above examples, in order to clearly distinguish the semantic classes and at the same time to show their basic correspondence with grammatical classes, there is no "skewing" between the semantic class and the grammatical class. That is to say, the Things listed are all represented by nouns, the Events by verbs, the Attributes by modifiers of some sort (adjectives, adverbs, affixes), and the Relations by prepositions and conjunctions. In the full lexicon and in the surface-structure representation of discourse concepts in any language, instances of skewing will occur, as when a noun represents an Event, or a verb an Attribute.

b. *Situational classification.* It was pointed out above that the concept has both referential and situational aspects and that the former is the basis for the classification of a concept as T, E, A, or R. It is also possible, and useful, to classify a concept on the basis of its situational aspect. No taxonomy of situational classes has been elaborated for the present theory. However, such a system would undoubtedly correlate quite closely with the parameters of "value" and "potency" discussed above (section 5.2.1). Furthermore, the situational classification of concepts would have to be sensitive to the distinction between lexical and discourse concepts. Although there may be some lexical items that carry only a negative, or positive, or neutral connotation, most lexical items have a potential to be classified negatively, positively, and neutrally, depending on their collocations in different configurations of concepts.

c. *Structural classification.* It may be useful to distinguish between simple and complex concepts. A *simple concept* is one in which each component is related to the central component directly and with the relation of delimitation. For example, both "boy" and "tall boy" would be simple concepts, as diagrammed in figure 5.1. The "packaging" number of seven, or, more likely, the "packaging" range of three to nine, comes into play here. It is rare to find a concept that consists of a central component and more than eight or nine components related to it directly. Such a concept would be regarded as unnatural, i.e., overloaded; and some other way would be found to convey the meaning.

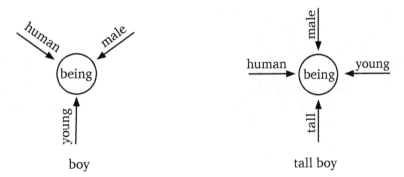

boy   tall boy

Figure 5.1. Simple concepts.

A *complex concept* is one in which there are components which are not directly related to the central component, but which are related to another component, usually with a relation other than a delimitational one. An example of such a concept would be "martyr." A martyr is a person who is put to death because he refuses to renounce his beliefs. Figure 5.2 shows this concept

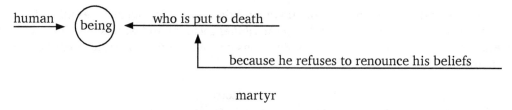

martyr

Figure 5.2. Complex concept.

diagrammed in the same way as "boy" and "tall boy." From the diagram it is clear that the component beginning with "because" is related to the component "who is put to death," giving a reason for it. Hence, "martyr" would be a complex concept.

A different example would be "baker." A baker can be defined as a person who bakes bread and sells it in order to make his living. (A wife who bakes bread and sells some of it to her neighbors as a service to them would not be called a baker.) This would be diagrammed as in figure 5.3.

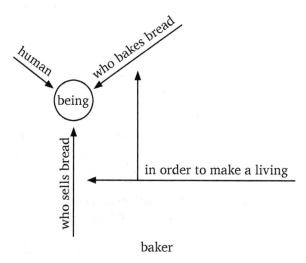

baker

Figure 5.3. Complex concept.

5.3.2 The external coherence of the concept

As a unit of discourse, the concept serves as a constituent of the proposition. As such, it relates to other concepts through a system of *case* relations. Thus, a concept may function as the central component of a proposition or as· any of a number of case roles, determined by the kind of proposition and the specific role that the concept is playing in that proposition. (For detailed presentation of the system of case relations, see figures 6.2 and 6.3.)

While we will not discuss the full implications of the following, suffice it to say that, whereas Thing, Event, and Attribute concepts commonly function as constituents of propositions, fulfilling specific case roles, Relation concepts serve to relate other concepts and do not themselves fill a case role in the proposition. In other words, in communication, Thing, Event, and Attribute concepts are related by Relation concepts to a central concept within the proposition.

5.3.3 The thematic content and purpose of the concept

The purpose of a concept is to refer to or identify a segment of the "world" that an author wants to talk about. When we ask what a concept is, we are getting very close to asking how people think and how they observe and see things around them. One way to describe a concept would be: "A concept is the product of that process whereby a Thing, an Event, an Attribute, or a Relation is isolated and distinguished from other Things, Events, Attributes, and Relations for purposes of reference." This is why different cultures have different concepts. They observe the world around them and they isolate from it that which they want to talk about, that which is relevant to their culture; and so there are differences of concepts from language to language.

Given that the purpose of the concept is to refer to a particular segment of the referential realm, it follows then, that all things being equal, the entire group of components would be significant to the achievement of that purpose and might therefore be regarded as "thematic." Technically, however, a thematic abstract or "theme" of the concept would consist of the most generic component, optionally delimited by one or more of the more generic specifying components.

It has been pointed out that marked prominence on a noncentral component of a concept will result in a highlighting of that component resulting in a diminishing of the prominence of other components (including the central one), even to the extent of the virtual cancellation of the other components. In such cases, the thematic content of those concepts would consist mainly in the highlighted component, and the other components would be regarded as incidental, or nonthematic.

5.4 The Concept and Surface Structure

Although there is a very close connection between the lexical concept and the grammatical morpheme and word, this does not mean that the discourse concept (or for that matter, the lexical concept) will be a single morpheme or word, or that it cannot be represented by several words. Consider the following examples:

> T - dancer, runner, single lady, three black cats
> E - to discourage, heighten, to go down, to go inside
> A - inconsiderate, thoughtless, more quickly, through the nose, in a discreet manner
> R - inside, as a result, in consequence

Notice, too, that the central component of the concept does not necessarily coincide with the nuclear morpheme of the word. In "dancer," for example, the nuclear morpheme is *dance*, with *-er* a nominalizing suffix. But semantically it is classed as a Thing, the generic component being a "being (human)," and this is represented not by the grammatical nucleus but by the *-er* suffix. Notice, also, that "concept clusters" may also have either a single-word or multiple-word representation in the same language or in different languages. In English, for example, a "single lady" can be expressed as "spinster"; "to go down" as "to descend"; "to go inside" as "to enter"; "more quickly" can also be expressed as "quicker"; "through the nose" is equivalent to "exorbitantly"; "in a discrete manner" is a longer form of "discretely"; "as a result" is the same as "therefore" in certain contexts, and so also is "in consequence"; etc.

There appears to be a significant correlation between the semantic classes and the grammatical classes. If, as described above, these are matched in a communication, then that communication will be more readily understood. If, on the other hand, there is a mismatch, or skewing, the communication is less easily understood. Even though this is true, skewing benefits the common process in a number of ways. There are advantages such as brevity and ease of handling prominence and topicalization. Skewing also adds "spice" to keep the addressee on his toes, to make the content more interesting, and to make the message more readily retained in the memory. If there were not such benefits from skewing, it would seldom occur. Skewing is exemplified by a Thing not being represented by a noun, an Event not represented by a verb, etc. A widespread example of skewing is the abstract noun—a noun which represents a concept that is not a Thing. For example:

> *salvation* represents the Event "to save"
> *height* represents the Attribute "high"
> *the reason* represents the Relation "because"

Another type of skewing occurs when an Attribute is represented by a verb, as in a number of West African languages; e.g., "she beautifuls," "it heavies," "it reds."

One important reason for the occurrence of skewing is that the topic of discussion is introduced in many languages, including English and Greek, in the form of a noun or noun phrase. Since we not only want to talk about Things but also about Events and Attributes (and in talking about the structure of language, Relations also), the nominalization of Events, Attributes, or Relations may be one surface-structure device used to indicate that an Event, an Attribute, or a Relation is now serving as topic.

Concepts are not merely equatable with the words of a language. While it is true that the inventory of lexical concepts represents potential discourse concepts, yet only as lexical items are used in context does it become clear whether they function as a concept or as part of a concept. An author may have available a word which only partially represents the concept to which he wants to refer. In such cases, the author will elaborate the basic concept until he arrives at the discourse concept he has in mind. In such instances, more than one word represents a single concept. It is useful, therefore, to illustrate some of the different surface-structure forms in which a concept may appear.

A concept may be further specified with a separate word as in "old man." Here "man" is described with the addition of "old," and when these two are combined in context, we have a single concept represented. There is still a single head component, a Thing, even though now we are dealing with a grammatical phrase rather than a single word. In "ran quickly," the Event concept "ran" is further modified with a concept which describes the manner of the running, but it is still an Event that is being referred to. A Thing concept may be further specified with an embedded proposition, which may take the form of a relative clause, or an abstract adjective. For example, in "The man who lives next door to us has just bought a puppy," the relative clause "who lives next door to us" represents an embedded proposition which describes the man and identifies which man has just bought a puppy. The proposition, therefore, may serve in the same way as a single concept or component does in the formation of a discourse concept. In the statement "he is a loving father," "loving" is an abstract adjective representing the embedded proposition, "who loves his children," which describes the central constituent "father." In all these examples, the central component remains unchanged. All the other components help to delimit more precisely the concept the author or speaker has in mind and wishes to talk about.

5.5 Summary

A concept is the product of that cognitive process whereby some segment of a referential world is isolated and distinguished from other segments for purposes of thought or reference.

A concept is a combination of components of meaning manifested in surface structure as a morpheme, a word, a sequence of words (phrase), or a word modified by one or more phrases or clauses.

A concept combines semantically compatible components of meaning. One of these components is central, and all the others are related to it directly by the delimitation relations (i.e., description or identification) or indirectly by the communication relations (in the case of complex concepts). The description or identification may be in the form of an embedded proposition.

The central component is naturally prominent and is the basis of which a concept is classified referentially as T, E, A, or R. Other components may be marked as prominent by special devices in the context.

In addition to the referential function, the concept also has a role function. A concept not only refers to a T, E, A, or R, it also takes on a specific role in a proposition such as Agent, Affectant, Owner, Location, etc. (These role functions are more fully treated in the next chapter.)

ANALYTICAL FEATURES	**UNITY:** Several components of meaning are combined to form what is conceptualized as a single segment of the referential world or communication situation	**INTERNAL COHERENCE:** The components of meaning are semantically compartible in the referential world and are appropriately related by delimitation relations to the central component.	**PROMINENCE:** One structural and relationally determined component of meaning is central, with or without contextually determined marked focus on it or any other component.
HOLISTIC FEATURES	**CLASS:** Based on the central referential component, it is a Thing, Event, Attribute, or Relation. Based on its connotational overtones, it may be subclassified as to value and potency.	**EXTERNAL COHERENCE:** It may serve as the central concept in a proposition; or any of the noncentral roles, such as Agent, Affectant, Classified, Owned, etc.	**THEMATIC CONTENT:** It refers to a particular segment of the referential world and expresses an appropriate connotation.

Figure 5.4. The meaning features of the concept.

6

THE PROPOSITION

The proposition is the smallest of the communication units; all other communication units are combinations of propositions—i.e., propositional configurations. Like other semantic units, the proposition involves the interplay of the three aspects of meaning—referential, situational, and structural. Because of this, it may be viewed from each of these perspectives.

6.1 Referential Meaning and the Proposition

From the referential standpoint, the proposition can be described as a semantic unit consisting of concepts, one being central and the others being directly related to it through a system of case relations. Two different types of proposition can then be distinguished on the basis of the classification of the central concept. If the central concept is an Event concept, then the proposition is an Event proposition; if the central concept is a Thing or Attribute concept, then the proposition is a State proposition.

6.1.1 State propositions

A State proposition, in its most basic form, consists of two concepts linked by some specific case relation. The central concept is the "state" and the other concept the "statant." Because the basic State proposition consists of these two concepts, the one that is the statant coincides with the topic; and the concept that is the state, together with the relation, constitutes the comment. (Any further optional concepts, such as those giving the time or the location of the State proposition, would also be part of the comment.)

a. *Types of State propositions*. The classification of State propositions is based upon the relation that links the statant to the state. The different types are exemplified in figure 6.1. (The propositions listed by Fleming (1978) have been very helpful in formulating the system.) It can be seen from the examples given in figure 6.1 that the relation may be represented in the surface structure by either of the two generic verbs "is" and "has," or by a more specific verb such as "own(s)," "belongs to," "contains," "comes from." These more specific verbs signal the relation precisely. In the case of the two generic verbs "is" and "has," the relation may be more precisely specified by expressions such as "is about," "is part of," "has…in it," or the relation may be deduced from the content of the statant and state concepts themselves. Thus, in "He is a doctor," the "is" signals only that a State relation exists between the two Things, "he" and "doctor," and it is from the content of the two concepts that the specific relation is known. (In other languages, some of the types of State propositions do not use a verb at all.)

Type of State Proposition	Example	Statant	State
naming	My dog is called "Fido"	my dog	"Fido"
	Her name is "Jennifer"	her	"Jennifer"
identification	That is a torque wrench	that	torque wrench
	The director is Jennifer	the director	Jennifer
description (attribution)	He is sick	he	sick
	She is tall	she	tall
substance	That table is made of wood	that table	wood
depiction	The story is about Bill	the story	Bill
ownership (possession)	That car is mine	that car	mine*
	That car belongs to me	that car	me
	I own that car	that car	I
partitive	The branch is part of a tree	the branch	a tree
	The tree has a trunk	the tree	a trunk
location	The car is in the garage	the car	the garage
	The car is outside the house	the car	the house
containership	This bag has rice in it	this bag	rice
	This bag contains rice	this bag	rice
derivation	Milk comes from cows	milk	cows
kinship role	She is my sister	she	my sister
social role	He is a doctor	he	a doctor
function	The room is for storage only	the room	storage
classification	A dog is an animal	a dog	an animal
	Red is a color	red	a color
ambience	It is hot	(ambience)	hot
	It is dark	(ambience)	dark
time	It is noon	(time)	noon
	It is 8 o'clock	(time)	8 o'clock
existence	God exists	God	exists
	There is sufficient evidence	sufficient evidence	there is

*The word "mine" represents both the Thing concept "I" and the relation of possession.

Figure 6.1. Types of State propositions.

Notice, however, that in many cases (probably all) these generic verbs can be replaced by more specific ones:

social role	He *works* as a doctor.
identification	That *is identified* as a torque wrench.
location	The car *is located in* the garage.
kinship role	She *is related to* me as my sister.
classification	A dog *is classified* as an animal.

The use of the generic verbs "is" and "has" is an example of language economy. Instead of using several words, a single generic word is used where undue ambiguity does not result.

The question can be raised in connection with *ambience* as to whether there is a statant present or not. It is quite possible that "the atmosphere," "the air," or "the weather" could be supplied, but language economy and context enable the implicit statant to be unspecified and simply referred to as "it." Similarly, with *time*, the common form using "it" may be a shorthand way of saying "The time is noon." Certainly, in question form, it has to be explicit: "What time is it?" (The same could be said of ambience also: the corresponding question is "What is *the weather* like today?")

It should be clear from the above discussion that a surface-structure verb, such as "own" or "be made" may represent a relation, and this semantic function is considerably more significant to the translator than the grammatical form used in English to represent it. So, it is not said that this is an Event concept used as a relation, but rather that it is a verb form used to represent a relation. The semantic function which the verb in the clause represents determines its classification as a relation rather than as an Event.

State propositions such as "The door is open" are analyzed in a similar way. The verb "to open," when used in such clauses as "Open the door" and "He opened the door," represents an Event concept. In "The door is open" there is no focus on any action, process, or experience. Rather, the focus is on the condition or state of "the door." Consequently, it is not an Event proposition but a State proposition, with a central Attribute concept, "open."

The point to be stressed here is that higher consideration must be given to semantic function than to grammatical form. A State proposition will not have an Event concept central since an Event concept always involves an action, experience, or process; a State proposition never involves any of these as its structural center.

b. *Roles within State propositions.* On the basis of the content of the statant and state concepts and the relation between them, a *role* can be assigned to the statant and the state. Using the same order as in the list of types of State propositions (figure 6.1), figure 6.2 gives the specific case roles in State propositions.

Statant Role	State Role
Named	Name
Identified	Identification
Described	Description
Item	Substance
Depicted	Depiction
Owned	Owner
Owner	Owned
Whole	Part
Part	Whole
Located	Location
Container	Contained
Derivative	Derivation
Referent	Kinship Role
Referent	Social Role
Used	Use
Member	Class
(Time)	Time Specification
(Ambience)	Ambience Description
Existent	Existence

Figure 6.2. Case roles in State propositions.

6.1.2 Event propositions

a. *Types of Event propositions.* There are different kinds of Event concepts that may be central to a proposition. There may be *actions* (e.g., "run," "hit," "eat"), *experiences* (e.g., "smell," "see," "hear"), *processes* (e.g., "die," "become sour," freeze"). Experiences are limited to the activities of the five senses or to cognitive or psychological activities (e.g., "think," "covet"). Processes always represent a change of state, i.e., from one state of being or condition to another. It is possible to combine actions and processes into a single Event concept as, for example, in "He lengthened the cord," or "He caused Bill to become sad." Both of these are in fact "caused processes." Since "cause" can be superimposed not only on processes but on actions and experiences as well, the justification for an additional class of Event concepts involving cause is questioned. It seems preferable to consider "cause" as an optional feature, which yields subclasses of Event propositions. In all cases, however, whether the cause is related to an action, experience, or process Event, the resultant Event is classed as an action Event. There are thus three main types of Event propositions: actions, experiences, and processes.

b. *Roles within Event propositions.* The information and the relations within Event propositions indicate the role of the different concepts. Since Fillmore (1968) propagated the notion of underlying case relations, various case systems have appeared. The list of roles presented in figure 6.3 borrows heavily from Longacre (1976 and 1980), who has done extensive and innovative work in this area. This list in no way represents the last word on case. It is a relatively conservative system in terms of the number of roles posited. There have been systems with as few as three roles (Austin Hale in Longacre 1976:36–37) and others with as many as forty-five roles (Fleming 1978).

6.1.3 The composition of the proposition in terms of T, E, and A

a. *State propositions.* When State propositions are analyzed in terms of the Things (T) and Attributes (A) involved, they are found to have one of four basic patterns (see figure 6.4). Sentences of the sort "Swimming is an exercise," "Learning to type is difficult," "Stealing is bad," etc., appear to be State propositions with the pattern Event/Event (EE) or Event/Attribute (EA). The E (swimming, learning, stealing) is the statant and the E/A (exercise, difficult, bad) is the state. The underlying semantic structure of these could be expressed as "People swim. This is a way in which they exercise"; "People learn how to (they) type. This is difficult"; and "People steal. This is bad." It would be tempting to restate the first example simply as "When people swim, they exercise." Note, however, that when this is done, the focus is changed—swimming is no longer the topic. Also, the relationship has shifted from one of classification to one of circumstance. The suggested semantic restructuring retains both. "This" as topic refers anaphorically to the proposition "people swim." Thus, the topic has not been changed in the semantic restatement. The relation of classification has been retained with a specific generic relationship, which is typical of all classification. The semantic structure shows that there is actually a State proposition, which has an embedded proposition as topic. In the second example, "it" refers to "People learn how to type"; in the third "this" refers to "People steal." Hence, all three of these examples represent complex propositions in the semantic structure.

Role	Definition	Example
Agent	the animate or inanimate doer of an action	*He* ran down the street. *The water* ran down the street.
Causer	the animate or inanimate instigator of an Event or State	*He* tripped me. (= He caused that I trip.) *He* shortened the rope. (= He caused that the rope be shorter.) *Malaria* killed her. (= Malaria caused that she die.) *The earthquake* weakened the building. (= The earthquake caused that the building be weak.)
Affectant (Experiencer, Patient)	that which undergoes or is affected by an Event	*He* smelled the lasagna. *He* fell down. *She* became sad. He hit *the ball*. *The butter* melted.
Beneficiary	the animate or inanimate Thing that is advantaged or disadvantaged by the Event	She gave the book to *her mother*. He sold the car for *his friend*.
Accompanier	the animate or inanimate Thing that participates in close association with the agent, causer, or affectant in an Event	He went to the park with *his dog*. The ice cream melted along with *the butter*.
Resultant (Range, Product)	the product of an action	She wrote *a letter*. He built *a house*. She sang *a song*.
Source	the point of departure/origin of an action	He flew in from *Chicago*. She ran away from *home*.
Path (Location)	the spatial location in/through/along which motion takes place	He walked through *the park*.
Goal (Destination)	that toward which an action is directed	He prayed to *God*. He went to *the store*.
Instrument	the inanimate Thing used to carry out an action	He looked at the insect with *his magnifying glass*. She painted the mural with *a broom*.
Time	the temporal placement of an Event	She earned her degree in *1978*. He worked on the painting for *six years*.
Measure	the quantification of an Event	He prays *five times a day*. They widened the road by *twenty feet*.

Figure 6.3. Case roles in Event propositions.

Pattern	Type
A	Time, Ambience
AA	Classification of Attributes
TA	Description, Existence
TT	All other types of State propositions

Figure 6.4. Patterns of State propositions.

The semantic structure for each of these examples has been represented with two propositions. Since, so far as is known, this is true of all classificatory clauses which can be analyzed as EE and of all descriptive clauses analyzed as EA, these clauses are considered to be surface representations of two propositions, one embedded in the other.

b. *Event propositions.* Similarly, the basic patterns of Event propositions can be listed, and these, too, are found to be four in number (see figure 6.5). To any of these it is possible to add an Attribute of time, e.g., "today," "yesterday," "now," "at noon," etc. Hence an Event proposition can have the form EA, TEA, etc., but the addition of time and location (in most propositions) is optional.

Pattern

E	It is raining (action).
TE	He ran (action).
	He meditated (experience).
	It melted (process).
TET	He ate the food (action).
	He saw Bill (experience).
	The water became wine (process)
TETT	He gave the book to Bill (action).
	He hit it with a stick (action).
	He tasted the wine for the King (experience)

Figure 6.5. Patterns of Event propositions.

It follows from the preceding discussion of State and Event propositions that every State proposition contains a central Thing or Attribute concept, and every Event proposition a central Event concept. It might be asked, however, whether an Event proposition consisting only of an Event concept really exists. For example, "it is raining" may simply be an English surface form for "rain is falling," which would be TE. Similarly, "it is snowing" is equivalent to "snow is falling," also a TE. In semantic structure, therefore, it may always be necessary to have a T to have a proposition, so that there would be only three basic patterns for Event propositions. The same might be said of those State propositions which consist only of an A (see the discussions of "ambience" and "time" earlier).

6.1.4 Referential coherence in the proposition

It has already been made clear that a proposition is a combination of concepts. This combination exhibits referential coherence only if the combination is perceived (in the referential realm of the discourse) as a single action, experience, process, or state. Thus, the statement "He ran, hopped, and skipped along the path" is not a single proposition because running, hopping, and skipping are not generally perceived as a single action. However, a proposition may take the form "The men, women, and children all enjoyed the picnic," since only one experience is being affirmed—those in attendance represent different classes of people, but the experience is single.

Furthermore, the concepts which are combined in a proposition must not result in nonsense. There must be coherence, i.e., the concepts must be semantically compatible with one another. The coherence rules vary from language to language, but the expectation of coherence in a semantic unit is universal.

6.2 Situational Meaning and the Proposition

The situational classification of the proposition. So far, this discussion has looked at the proposition from the perspective of its referential meaning. A good deal of emphasis was placed on the referential classification of propositions. But now we want to ask the question, "What is the author trying to *do* with the referential meaning he is manipulating in the proposition?"

The answer to that question is known as the *illocutionary force* of the proposition, and, very generically, it is threefold: it may be to make a statement, to ask a question, or to give a command. Every proposition can be classed as belonging to one of these three broad illocutionary classes.

Both Event and State propositions may occur with any of these three illocutionary forces, but commanded States only occur with the general meaning of "Maintain the state you are in," as in "Continue to be faithful to God"; "Sit there!" (the child is already sitting at the time of the command); and "Leave the door open."

As more specific classifications are given to propositions, a caution to be sounded concerning the necessity of maintaining a clear distinction between the situational (illocutionary) class of the information and the structural (relational) class of the information. For example, in the propositional configuration "He stayed at home because it was raining," both propositions belong to the situational class of affirmative statements. But classed by structural, or role, information, the first proposition is a "result" proposition and the second is a "reason" proposition.

An analogy can be drawn with concepts. Concepts are classified as Things, Events, Attributes, or Relations. The concept also has a role in the proposition, e.g., as Agent, Affectant, Instrument, Owner, etc. The role information must be ignored in assigning the referential and situational classification of the concept. The same procedure is followed with propositions. Thus, in principle, a support proposition may belong to any one of the three situational (illocutionary) classes proposed for independent propositions.

Mood has been referred to as a situational perspective that is inherent in a proposition (sections 2.1.2 and 2.3.2). This is because illocutionary force is inherent in all propositions and mood is the primary indicator of illocutionary force, though not the only one. The illocutionary perspective may be signaled implicitly, or explicitly by mood or a speech orienter. Consider the following three (simple) examples, which represent the illocutionary force by *mood*:

Go.	(command)
He went.	(statement)
Why did he go?	(question)

In the first example, the illocutionary force of command is shown by the absence of a subject, the non-third person form of the verb, and the present tense ("went," "will go," etc., cannot form imperatives). The last example is shown to be a question by the presence of a question word, the verb being put in auxiliary form, and the reversal of order between auxiliary and subject pronoun (cf. "Yes, he did go" for the statement order). In the following examples, however, the illocutionary force is indicated by a speech orienter:

I command that you go.
I say that he went.
I ask why did he go?

In some languages, such as European ones, there are many specific speech orienters which serve to signal finer distinctions. Commands, questions, and statements can be expressed with various degrees of certainty, authority, intensity, delicacy, etc., as illustrated in figure 6.6.

STATEMENT	COMMAND	QUESTION
say	demand	ask
exclaim	urge	demand
shout	request	wonder
whisper	desire	inquire
etc.	etc.	etc.

Figure 6.6. Specific speech orienters.

In addition, all speech orienters can be further subdivided according to whether the speaker orientation is first person present tense, or not. First person present tense speaker orientations are called *performatives*—I say, etc. Speech orienters other than first person present tense are called *reportatives*—He said, etc. Figure 6.7 gives the various possibilities.

ILLOCUTIONARY FORCE	PERFORMATIVE	REPORTATIVE
Statement	I say	They say, I said, etc.
Command	I command	He commands, I commanded, etc.
Question	I ask	He asks, you asked, etc.

Figure 6.7. Speech orienters and illocutionary force.

It is clear, then, that mood and orienters play an important part in providing a basis for the classification of propositions as statements, commands, or questions. Other factors are time, aspect, polarity, tone, and register. These further factors lead to an extensive range of more specific classifications, which are detailed in chapter 2 (2.3.2).

6.3 Structural Meaning and the Proposition

6.3.1 The structural role of the proposition

When a proposition is considered in terms of its distribution, it is possible to identify a role that it plays in the larger semantic context. It may be serving as a head proposition in a propositional configuration; it may be an Orienter; it may have one of a number of support or stimulus roles—e.g., Reason, Means, Occasion, etc. These role functions will be treated more fully when the relations and roles of communication units are discussed in chapter 8.

6.3.2 Relational coherence in the proposition

The concepts within a proposition must not only be referentially compatible with one another (see 6.1.4 above), but they must also be appropriately related. That is, they must be semantically compatible with and appropriate for the relations that link them, thus forming a coherent whole. The case relations serve this function. For example, the concepts "the monkey," "climbed rapidly," and "the tree" are semantically compatible (i.e., they have referential coherence). If they are related together in the proposition "The monkey rapidly climbed the tree," then "the monkey" appropriately fills the role of Agent; "climbed rapidly" appropriately fills the role of the central action concept; and "the tree" fills the role of Path. "The tree" could not serve as the Agent; nor could the Path for climbing be "the monkey" or "in the air." The statement would be incoherent, i.e., hard to conceptualize in any referential world, which is what is meant by nonsense.

6.3.3 Prominence and structural meaning

Earlier, it was said that a proposition consists of a topic and a comment, looked at from an information-structure perspective. What is being talked about is called the *topic*; what is being said about it is called the *comment*.

The topic, though not the most naturally prominent part of the proposition, is considered to be quite integral to the thematic content of the proposition because it is what is being talked about—without a topic there could be no communication. The comment is the most naturally prominent part of the structure of the proposition because it is the "new" information, that which the author wants to communicate about the topic. Also, the referential center of the proposition, the central Event, Thing, or Attribute concept, is normally found in the comment. Probably, more strictly speaking, it is not the *whole* comment that is naturally prominent, but the central concept.

While each proposition may be analyzed as a topic/comment combination, the topic of any proposition does not take on any higher-level significance until that proposition occurs in a sequence of propositions and one topic from several topics is clearly seen to be the topic of the sequence.

a. *Natural topics.* Topics may be natural or marked. In Event propositions, if the Event concept is an action, then the natural topic will be the Thing concept that does the action, i.e., the Agent, Affectant, or Causer. In cases where there is both an Agent and Affectant (e.g. "He (Agent) hit me (Affectant)"), the Agent is naturally prominent. In English (and Greek), the natural topic is most often encoded by, or represented by, the "subject" in the surface form. (In the following examples, the topic is italicized.)

He threw the ball a long way.	(Agent)
The boy fell asleep.	(Affectant)
She made the child eat his dinner.	(Causer)

If the Event concept is an experience, then the natural topic is the Thing concept with the role of Affectant:

He saw a large snake.	(Affectant)

Where the Event concept is a process, then the natural topic is the Thing concept with the role of Affectant:

The butter melted	(Affectant)
The rope steadily lengthened.	(Affectant)
I fell over.	(Affectant)
He died.	(Affectant)

Each example above is a statement. The topic in the corresponding questions would be represented by the question word replacing the subject, e.g., *Who* fell asleep? *Who* made the child eat his dinner? *What* melted? Etc.

b. *Marked topics.* A marked topic is any Thing concept which is the topic, but not a natural topic as defined above. In other words, a concept is considered to be a marked topic when its role in the proposition is not one of those listed for a natural topic. For example, in any type of proposition if the Instrument is the topic, then it is a marked topic, as in "The iron bar shattered the window." Or, if an Affectant concept in an action proposition is the topic, as in "A prize will be presented to the student with the best grades," then that Affectant concept ("a prize") is the marked topic. Beneficiary is like Instrument; if it occurs as the topic, in any sort of proposition, then it is a marked topic. An example would be "The President's wife was presented with a beautiful bouquet of flowers by a little girl," where the Beneficiary is "the President's wife."

In all of the above examples, the natural topic is a Thing. But it is not at all unusual to find such statements as "*His height* is a great advantage," or "*His diligence in studying* is well known," or "*His piano playing* is outstanding." In the first of these examples, "his height" represents the State proposition, "he is tall." In the second, "his diligence in studying" represents the Event proposition "he studies diligently." And in the third, "his piano playing" represents the Event proposition "he plays the piano." In each case, the underlying proposition has been nominalized in the surface structure   which is the surface form of topics in many languages—and made the topic of a State proposition; i.e., each of these (nominalized) topics is an embedded proposition in the semantic structure. These, too, are considered to be marked topics. The same is true for embedded propositions which are the topics in Event propositions; so, all embedded propositions (or even larger communication units) which are topics are regarded as marked topics.

A topic may also be marked by using some appropriate prominence device of the language. One such device in Greek and English is the passive voice. In the following examples, it is the Affectant that is marked as the topic by making it the subject of a passive verb.

> *The flowers* were given to Betty by Bill.
> *He* was guarded by six soldiers.

c. *Topic and comment in commands.* It has been stated that the central concept of a proposition is never the topic since the central concept is always part of the comment. However, it is by no means certain that this general pattern holds in the case of commands. The problem does not arise with statements and questions because the former are imparting information on a topic, and the latter are requesting information about some topic, or requesting to know what the topic is. But in a command, such as *stand up* or *bring me the screwdriver,* it is not immediately clear what the topic is. It is true, "you" is understood as the subject of the verb, but nothing is said about "you," i.e., "you" is not the topic. Rather, "you" identifies the one being addressed. It would appear that the natural topic of transitive commands is represented by the object of the verb (i.e., the concept with the role of Affectant), and that the natural topic of intransitive commands is represented by the verb itself (i.e., the Event concept). It would seem, therefore, that the topic/comment distinction is valid for all three illocutionary classes, but that that structure varies with the different classes.

6.4 Prominence and the Three Aspects of Meaning in the Proposition

In has been shown that, *referentially,* the proposition consists of a grouping of concepts in which one is central and the others directly or indirectly related to it. The naturally prominent referential content of a proposition is the central Event, Thing, or Attribute concept, the hub of the proposition. *Structurally,* it has been shown how the topic and comment are significantly involved in the thematic content of the proposition, with the comment being the most prominent part. Natural versus marked topics have been distinguished, the latter being the result of what might be called "topicalization." Some of the differences of natural prominence due to the various *situational* (illocutionary) perspectives of propositions have been pointed out.

In addition to these prominence features, *marked prominence* may be given to any concept (or more than one) in a proposition by means of the surface-structure prominence devices. As noted in connection with the concept, four types of marked prominence are distinguished: contrastive focus, all-inclusive focus, intensive focus, and highlighting (section 5.2.3). Note the following examples:

Contrastive Forms:	*Bill, not John,* mowed the lawn.
All-inclusive Focus:	She took *her whole family—parents, grandparents, brothers and sisters, cousins, etc.*—to the amusement park.
Intensive Focus:	*Billy himself* was invited.
Highlighting:	*It was her Uncle Walt* she forgot to invite.

It is important to note that marked prominence can be added to the natural topic. For example:

> *It was Bill* who gave her the flowers.

Bill was the one who gave her the flowers.

In these two examples, "Bill" is the natural topic (Agent of an action). Marked prominence is added and expressed in the first instance with "It was…who," and in the second with "was the one who."

It is also important to note that marked prominence can occur more than once in the same proposition. Consider the statement:

It was a kite that Bob *himself* gave to the child.

In this statement, "a kite" is the highlighted Affectant, and within the comment, the intensifying pronoun "himself" adds marked prominence to the Agent "Bob." In Greek, highlighting is commonly shown by word order, as, for example, in Rom. 13:1c. The Greek could be translated "those that exist have been instituted by God," but where English would use phonological features to highlight "God," Greek places the phrase "by God" before the verb. Note the complexity of this example. The passive voice has been used to topicalize the Affectant "those that exist," and word order has been used to highlight the Agent, so that this one statement exhibits two different examples of marked prominence, using two different devices.

Prominence, therefore, in a proposition, consists of the interplay between the central referential concept, the topic/comment structure, and any of the optional marked prominence features listed above.

Before we leave the complex subject of prominence and the three aspects of meaning, one special case merits some further discussion. As pointed out above, in an intransitive command, the verb itself represents the topic. The command may be represented in the surface structure by a nominal phrase, and forefronted. This is a way to indicate highlighting prominence on the natural topic. An example of this is found in Col. 4:2 where the Greek reads *tē proseuchē proskartereite* 'with-respect-to-prayer be-persevering'. Since the Event *to pray* is both nominalized and forefronted, it is analyzed as being a highlighted topic.

6.5 The Proposition and Surface Structure

The impression may have been left in the discussion so far that propositions are equivalent to surface-structure clauses (or their equivalent forms). This is only true in the sense that the clause is the most neutral, or matched, representation that can be given to a proposition in a natural language. In fact, a word or phrase may also be used to represent a proposition. In Greek, the various surface structure forms which may represent the central Event concept of an Event proposition are:

1. Finite verbs
2. Infinitives
3. Participles
4. Abstract nouns
5. Elided verbs (commonly in comparisons and contrasts)
6. Implied verbs (in such prepositional phrases as "in Christ" or "for Christ"; and in genitive constructions such as "the God of me," "a prisoner of Christ," "traditions of you").

State propositions are frequently represented by adjectives, and various types of noun phrases ("my car," "a bag of beans," "the red wagon," etc.).

A knowledge of the different surface-structure forms by which a central Event concept may be represented in a specific language is an essential prerequisite to the analysis procedure. (Event propositions are much more common than State propositions in written discourse, so the main interest here is in the surface form of Event propositions.)

Why does the Event proposition appear in so many different forms? It has been observed that the finite form of the verb appears in all known languages. On the other hand, there are languages that do not have participles and infinitives, and the use of abstract nouns and ellipsis varies in languages both as to when they may be used and how often. So it appears that the finite form of the verb is basic, i.e., it represents the full, surface-structure form which underlies abbreviated surface forms, such as participles, infinitives, abstract nouns, etc.; and at the same time the finite verb gives the least ambiguous representation of the semantic structure.

Language tends toward packing as much information as possible into the smallest possible stretch of forms. This, then, is one reason why a proposition, whose unabridged surface form is represented by a finite verb clause, may also be represented in the surface structure by nonfinite verb clauses, noun phrases, and even abstract nouns.

At the same time, not everything that is said is of equal importance. The speaker desires to give prominence to, or at least to make obvious, what his main point is. This is frequently accomplished by communicating the supporting information in a form other than a finite verb.

6.6 Representing the Proposition in a Semantic Structure Analysis

In the light of the above discussion dealing with the relationship between the surface structure and the semantic structure, certain principles or procedures can now be stated concerning the representation of the proposition in a semantic-structure analysis.

REFERENTIAL	SITUATIONAL	STRUCTURAL

Action: hit
Agent: Bill
Patient: ball
Instrument: bat
 	
(more specifically, Bill
= [being, human, adult, name:
Bill, role: Agent])
	illocution: statement
	polarity: positive
	situational time: two
	  hours after the refer-
	  ential time
	speaker authority:
	  eyewitness
	etc.
		Topic: Bill
		old information: Bill
		focal information: ball
		nonfocal information:
		  Instrument: bat
		etc.

Figure 6.8. The strict representation of a proposition.

A *strict representation* would be one free of the surface-structure constraints of any given language. It would be a constellation of semantic properties including each of the aspects of meaning. Something like that in figure 6.8 would result.

For practical reasons, an alternative method of representing the semantic analysis of a proposition has been developed. It involves the verbalization of the analysis using English surface structure, but with certain restrictions. The restrictions are as follows:

1. The grammatical classes and the semantic classes match each other, i.e., all Events are verbal forms, Things are nouns or pronouns, Attributes are adverbs or adjectives, and Relations are conjunctions, prepositions, case markers, or word order.

2. The finite form of the verb is normally used.

3. The natural topic is expressed by the subject position of the clause; a marked topic is expressed either by forefronting or by occurrence in the subject position in addition to the passive form of the verb.

4. For any Event concept, all its obligatory roles are stated.

5. Implicit information, such as the point of similarity of similes and metaphors, is stated.

6. Only the primary senses of English words are used to verbalize semantic notions.

7. All figures, except similes and live metaphors, are expressed in a nonfigurative way. (Special notations will sometimes be used to indicate the type of figure that was used in the surface structure of the source text.)

These principles are exemplified below from part of Col. 1:9:

Prop. 1   we have been praying (to God) for you very frequently [LITOTES]

Grk. A	*ou*	*pauometha*	*huper*	*humōn*	*proseuchomenoi*
	not	we-cease	for	you	praying

Prop. 2   and we have been asking (God)

Grk. B	*kai*	*aitoumenoi*
	and	asking

Prop. 3   that (God) would cause that you know thoroughly

Grk. C	*hina*	*plērōthēte*	*tēn*	*epignōsin*
	that	you-might-be-filled-with	the	knowledge

Prop. 4   which he [God] wills

Grk. D	*tou*	*thelēmatos*	*autou*
	of-the	will	of-him

Each of the principles listed above is illustrated in this example as follows:

1. There is considerable skewing between the surface classes and the semantic classes. The Attributes "frequently" in Proposition 1 and "thoroughly" in Proposition 3 are both represented by finite verbs (*pauometha* (A) and *plērōthēte* (C) respectively), and the Events "know" in Proposition 3 and "wills" in Proposition 4 are represented by the nouns *epignōsin* (C) and *thelēmatos* (D).

2. The surface participles in A and B (*proseuchomenoi* and *aitoumenoi*) become finite verbs in Propositions 1 and 2. In Proposition 3 the construction "cause you *to know*" is avoided, as it uses an infinitive.

3. The natural topic in Propositions 1 and 2 is "we," which is the case also in the Greek. Surface form C is complex because of the causative Event expressed by the passive *plērōthēte* 'you might be filled'. The passive form also signals the topicalization of "you." The Causer, God, has been expressed overtly (in parentheses) in Proposition 3 (fulfilling principle 4) and the topicalization of "you" is carried by making it the subject of the noun clause "that *you* know thoroughly." In phrase D, there is no verb form, but the Event "wills" corresponds with the abstract noun *thelēmatos* 'will'. This is part of a genitive construction, in which the pronoun *autou* 'of him' represents the Agent of the (nominalized) Event "to will" and also the topic of the corresponding Proposition 4.

4. Examples of principle 4 are found in Propositions 1 and 2 where the Events "pray" and "ask" both require the role of Goal, so this has been supplied in parentheses.

5. The Goal supplied in Propositions 1 and 2 is an example of implicit information made explicit.

6. Principle 6 is illustrated by the use of "cause...thoroughly" instead of the common, more literal rendering of *plērōthēte* with "be filled." For "fill" to fit this passage, it would have to be understood in a nonprimary sense; so it is replaced with an expression whose primary sense fits the semantic context.

7. The opening two words in A, *ou pauometha* 'we do not cease', are an example of litotes, i.e., a double negation for highlighting the corresponding positive concept. This has been expressed nonfiguratively by modifying the adverb "frequently" with the intensifier "very." Also the figure has been identified in brackets following the proposition.

6.7 Summary

The proposition is a combination of concepts which states, questions, or commands an Event or State and which is organized in a topic-comment structure.

A proposition characteristically relates to other propositions, or configurations of propositions, by means of the communication relations, and has a communication role. (See chapter 8 for a detailed discussion of communication relations and roles.) A proposition may, however, relate to a concept, in which case it is embedded, and has a delimitational role, either of Description or Identification.

ANALYTICAL FEATURES	UNITY: Concepts combine to form what is conceptualized as a single Event or State in the referential world.	INTERNAL COHERENCE: Concepts which are semantically compatible relate appropriately through a system of case relations.	PROMINENCE: One (or more) of the concepts is structurally central, being supported by concepts in obligatory roles and supplemented by concepts with marked focus.
HOLISTIC FEATURES	CLASS: Based on its referential content, it may be an Event or State; based on its situational content, it is a statement, command, or question.	EXTERNAL COHERENCE: It serves either as the head proposition in a propositional configuration; or as a support proposition with any of the communication roles; or to describe or identify a concept.	THEMATIC CONTENT: It communicates a particular statement, command, or question concerning a particular topic, thereby contributing to the theme and purpose of the unit of which it is a constituent.

Figure 6.9. The meaning features of the proposition.

7

THE PROPOSITIONAL CLUSTER

7.1 The propositional cluster as a propositional configuration

A propositional configuration may be defined as a combination of propositions or other propositional configurations, such that one of them is central and the others are directly related to it by means of a system of communication relations (see chapter 8). While this does describe the propositional configuration and clearly distinguishes it from the concept and the proposition, it could serve to describe any of the propositional configurations—propositional clusters, paragraphs, sections, divisions, etc. This is due to the recursive nature of the configuration, i.e., that a constituent of a configuration may be another configuration. This implies that every discourse consisting of more than one proposition is analyzable into a system of recursively intertwined propositional configurations and ultimately is reducible to a single propositional cluster. Figure 7.1 graphically illustrates this. Any of the combinations of propositions (1–2, 6–12, 13–18, 1–21, etc.) is a propositional configuration. Each is essentially identical to the others in terms of its constituents (propositions or propositional configurations) and the system of communication relations used to relate its constituents and to relate it to other propositions or configurations.

There are, however, two other factors that come into play to distinguish one propositional configuration from another: span cotermination and organizational level. The factor of *span cotermination* has to do with the interrelationship of the referential, situational, and structural spans of the discourse. A span may be defined as a portion of a discourse that is characterized by the high density of a particular feature or element of meaning. The limits of spans are set at those points of maximum variation in the density of the particular item under consideration. The feature or element of meaning may be referential, situational, or structural. For example, a stretch of text may be characterized by a high density of concepts from the experiential domain of fishing (e.g., fish, boat, sea, hook, nets, etc.), whereas prior to that stretch of text and immediately following it there is a very low density of occurrences of concepts from that particular domain. The high-density stretch of text would be a referential span.

By "cotermination" of spans is meant that one or both of the boundaries of more than one span occur at the same point in the discourse. For example, it may be that coterminous with the referential "fishing" span is a situational span consisting of the high-density occurrence of propositions with the illocutionary force of affirmative statement and a structural span consisting of a sequence of propositions with the same topic. These coterminous spans may be followed by other different ones, such as a referential span centering around the domain of wildlife conservation, a situational span characterized by the illocutionary force of command, and a structural span with "wildlife" as topic.

PROPOSITIONS CONFIGURATIONS

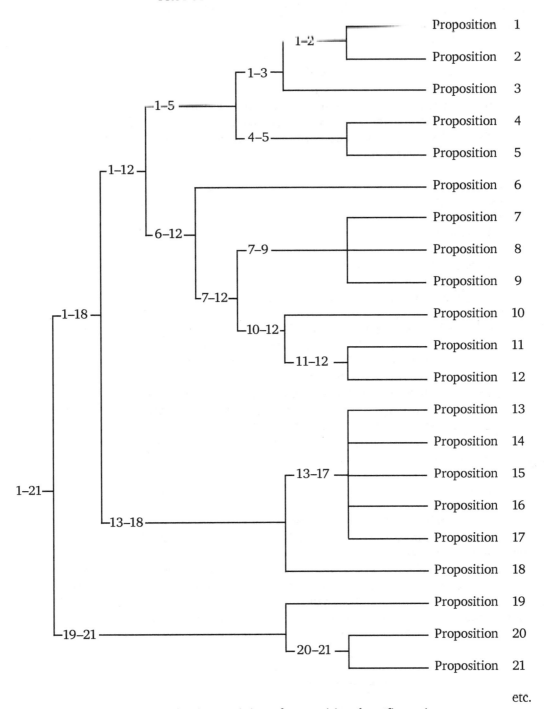

Figure 7.1. Recursive intertwining of propositional configurations.

The other criterion which functions to distinguish different kinds of propositional configurations is *organizational level*. Each unit in the semantic hierarchy consists of constituents. In general, propositional clusters consist of propositions; paragraphs consist of propositional clusters; sections consist of paragraphs; and so on. However, the flexibility of language is such that a propositional cluster (for example) may be a constituent of a section, along with paragraphs. Or it may be that a very complex propositional configuration that is larger than many paragraphs, might be analyzed as a propositional cluster within a paragraph along with other propositions and simple propositional clusters.

This last statement leaves unanswered two questions: (1) How were these two configurations identified as propositional clusters rather than as paragraphs?, (2) What is meant by saying one is a constituent of the section and the other of a paragraph? Are not all the various parts—the concepts, propositions, and propositional clusters—constituents? The second question is answered first. By *constituent* is meant a proposition or configuration which is directly related to the center of the unit of which it is a part. Every configuration, from the cluster to the total discourse, has a center to which everything else is related. But some of the configurations within a unit are *directly* related to its center; others are not, but are related *indirectly,* that is to say, they are related to a proposition or configuration other than the central one.

An example is probably the best way to make this clear. Consider the following paragraph from Col. 1:21–23 (adapted and simplified for this purpose). Each proposition has been written on a separate line and numbered consecutively.

(1)   Although you were formerly alienated from God
(2)   since you acted evilly
(3)   God has now reconciled you
(4)   by means of his Son dying physically
(5)   in order that you should be completely holy
(6)   when God brings you into his own presence
(7)   if you continue to believe the gospel
(8)   specifically, if you continue to be stable.

The central, or head, proposition is number 3; all the others are ultimately related to it. If, however, we consider in detail the ways in which the different propositions are related, we note that the first is related to the head itself, as can be seen by simply juxtaposing the two propositions: "(1). Although you were formerly alienated from God, (3) God has now reconciled you." Juxtaposed in this way, they make good sense. Proposition 2, on the other hand, is directly related to proposition 1; in this context, "since" means "as was shown by the fact that" It signals a unit that gives evidence in support of proposition 1—i.e., their alienation from God was evidenced by their evil deeds. Proposition 2 cannot be related directly to proposition 3; to do so would make nonsense. Proceeding in the same way, it soon becomes clear that propositions 4 and 5 relate back to proposition 3, explaining "how" God effected the reconciliation and what its "purpose" was. But proposition 6 provides information concerning the time of proposition 5, proposition 7 states a proviso to propositions 5 and 6, and proposition 8 gives a specific instance of proposition 7.

Propositions 1–8 constitute a paragraph, of which proposition 3 is clearly the center, since all the other propositions relate back to it. Proposition 1, 4, and 5, however, do so directly; so they enable us to identify the main constituents of this paragraph. The other propositions do so indirectly—i.e., through forming other propositional configurations.

So far, the paragraph has been discussed mainly in terms of propositions, which is a first step towards its analysis into propositional clusters. On the basis of what has been said above, the paragraph can be diagrammed as in figure 7.2. This diagram shows that the paragraph can be analyzed as consisting of four main "blocks" of information, one of which is the central block, with the other three directly related to it. These four blocks, then, are the main constituents of this paragraph.

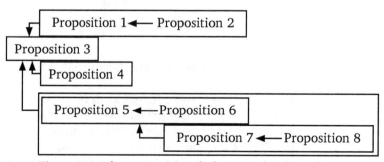

Figure 7.2. The propositional clusters of Col. 1:21–23.

Now, since paragraphs most commonly consist of propositional clusters, does it follow that all these four constituents of this paragraph are propositional clusters? It is obvious from the diagram that two of the constituents, the first and the last, consist of two or more propositions, whereas the central one and the third one do not; they consist of only one proposition each. We would then say that the first and last constituents are propositional clusters and that the second and third constituents are propositions, not clusters.

There is still the question as to how a propositional cluster and a paragraph would be distinguished if they were both constituents of a higher-level unit (e.g., a section). The guideline for making such a distinction, stated briefly, is that at the lower levels of the organization structure of a discourse, if a combination of two or more propositions is a constituent of a paragraph, then it is considered to be a propositional cluster, not a paragraph, even if it is very complex. Phlm. 13–14 provides a good illustration of a highly complex propositional cluster. These two verses are a constituent of one of the paragraphs in Philemon (12–16), and so, as stated above, are therefore analyzed as a propositional cluster. In figure 7.3 they are presented with a tree diagram showing the complex recursive relationship of the member propositions.

This large cluster, with its eleven member propositions, also illustrates the fact that there is a "fuzzy border" so far as size is concerned between a larger, complex cluster, such as the one above, and a small paragraph. If Phlm. 13–14 were a constituent of a section, there would be no hesitation in labeling it a paragraph; but in its present context, it is analyzed as a propositional cluster. In other words, the organizational level serves to distinguish the different propositional configurations. This "fuzzy-border" phenomenon arises at this point because of the recursive nature of propositional configurations, and is found at every level in the hierarchy from the propositional cluster upwards.

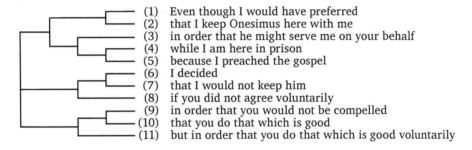

(1)	Even though I would have preferred
(2)	that I keep Onesimus here with me
(3)	in order that he might serve me on your behalf
(4)	while I am here in prison
(5)	because I preached the gospel
(6)	I decided
(7)	that I would not keep him
(8)	if you did not agree voluntarily
(9)	in order that you would not be compelled
(10)	that you do that which is good
(11)	but in order that you do that which is good voluntarily

Figure 7.3. Recursive relationship among member propositions of Phlm. 13–14.

7.2 Simple, complex, and compound propositional clusters

It is convenient, when talking about the propositional cluster, to have some way of referring to its various structures, as was done for the concept (section 5.3.1). The structure of a propositional cluster is said to be *simple* if every proposition of which it consists is directly related to the center proposition(s). It is said to be *complex* if some of the propositions of which it consists are only indirectly related to the center, i.e., they are related to propositions or configurations which are not central. The example from Philemon above is obviously complex. In the example above from Colossians (figure 7.2), the first cluster is simple, the last one is complex.

In simple propositional clusters, the supporting propositions may be independently related to the head proposition, each having a different supporting role; or they may all have the same role with respect to the head proposition, being related to one another by Conjoining. Consider, for example, figure 7.4. In this cluster, 2 is the head proposition, with 1 independently supporting it. But in figure 7.5, propositions 1 and 2 form a conjoined pair with the same supporting role with respect to the head, proposition 3.

```
┌─means─────── (1) By selling newspapers,
│
└─HEAD ─────── (2) he earned money.
```

Figure 7.4. Simple propositional cluster (A).

```
┌─means₁ ─────── (1) By selling newspapers
│
├─means₂ ─────── (2) and by washing windows,
│
└─HEAD──────── (3) he earned money.
```

Figure 7.5. Simple propositional cluster (B).

When a propositional cluster has more than one head proposition, it is said to be a *compound* propositional cluster. These also may be simple or complex. In compound propositional clusters that are simple, the heads are conjoined, and any supporting propositions relate equally to all of the heads. Consider the cluster in figure 7.6. In this unit, propositions 2 and 3 are conjoined heads, with proposition 1 supporting both of them.

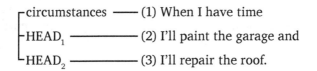

Figure 7.6. Compound propositional cluster–simple.

In compound clusters that are complex, there are propositions which support one, or more, but not all of the head propositions. Note the cluster in figure 7.7. In this one both head propositions (2 and 4) are independently developed, making this a compound cluster that is complex.

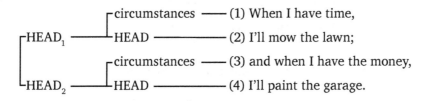

Figure 7.7. Compound propositional cluster–complex.

7.3 Coherence in the propositional cluster

Referential coherence is based on sameness of information—i.e., on recurrence of referential meaning and on concepts drawn from the same semantic or experiential domains within the unit being considered. In a simple propositional cluster, with only two propositions involved, it is probable that only the latter of these two types of referential coherence will occur; but, in general, there will be repeated reference to the same concepts by means of synonyms, anaphora, identical repetitions, etc. *Structural* coherence in the propositional cluster means primarily that the propositions and/or other configurations of which it consists are appropriately related to one another, given the referential world of the communication.

Consider, for example, the third constituent propositional cluster in Col. 1:21–23 discussed above (figure 7.2). It reads as follows:

(5)   ...you should be completely holy
(6)   when God brings you into his own presence

Referential coherence is shown by the repetition of "you" in both propositions and the fact that "holy" and "God's presence" are drawn from an experiential domain clearly recognized in the referential world spoken of in the Scriptures, in which all that is in God's presence is holy. It follows that the two propositions are compatible in this referential world and that the relation of Time between them is appropriate, as being brought into God's presence requires holiness in the object brought. This is an example of a simple cluster. In more complex clusters, there will generally be more evidence of referential and structural coherence.

7.4 Classification of the propositional cluster

With respect to classification, the propositional cluster does not differ from the proposition. This is because the classification of the cluster is based on the class of its head proposition(s). So, like the proposition, the generic classification is as a statement, question, or command. To this may be added the many subclassifications already presented in the overview (section 2.3.2).

7.5 The role and purpose of the propositional cluster

A propositional cluster has a role function determined by the part it plays in the relational structure of the unit of which it is a constituent (typically in a paragraph). It may be the head cluster or one of the other constituent clusters functioning as a Reason, Means, Specific, etc., in support of the head cluster. It may also function as an Occasion, Proposal, etc., in narrative genre. These different roles will be discussed in detail in the next chapter.

Likewise, the purpose of the propositional cluster is not essentially different from that of the proposition. Its content contributes towards the purpose that is established for the higher-level unit of which the cluster is a constituent. However, when the propositional cluster is a constituent of a high-level unit such as a division, it is likely to have its own clearly discernable and somewhat self-sufficient purpose.

7.6 Prominence in the propositional cluster

As has been mentioned earlier in this chapter (section 7.1), the propositional cluster has a center to which all its member propositions are related directly or indirectly. This center will normally be a single proposition; but if there is an Orienter proposition, the center may consist of the Orienter and its Content. An instance of this occurs in the example from Philemon (figure 7.3). The center of this propositional cluster is "I decided that I would not keep him." This consists of the cognitive Orienter "I decided" and its Content "that I would not keep him." The central (Head) proposition of the cluster constitutes the *naturally* prominent part of the cluster.

In addition, any proposition in a propositional cluster can have *marked* prominence, but at this level in the hierarchy there appears to be only highlighting focus, i.e., a proposition is picked out as prominent by special surface-structure devices. If a proposition which is directly related to the center proposition(s) has marked prominence, then it is added to the Head, and together they form the prominent information in that cluster.

Since the center of a propositional cluster is a proposition, it follows from the discussion of the proposition (section 6.3.3) that there is a main *topic* and a main *comment* in a propositional cluster, i.e., the topic and comment of the main proposition, i.e., the topics of the noncentral propositions may be the same as the main topic, or they may differ. In the first propositional cluster of Col. 1:21–23 (figure 7.2), the topic is the same in both propositions, i.e., "you." In the more complex example from Philemon (figure 7.3), the main topic is "I," but there is one proposition where the topic is "he" (proposition 3), and the configuration consisting of propositions 8–11 has the topic "you."

7.7 The propositional cluster and surface structure

In the surface structure, a propositional cluster may be represented by a clause, a sentence, or a group of clauses within a sentence. In Greek, with which the Bible translator is particularly concerned, it is possible to make a distinction between the form a propositional cluster takes in epistolary and narrative material. In narration, such as in the Gospels and Acts, it is more common for the propositional cluster to be represented by a sentence. In the epistles, on the other hand, a clause or group of clauses is often used. This is especially true in those epistles where the sentences tend to be very long.

This broad generalization, however, will not invariably hold true. Even in the epistles, the propositional cluster is quite often represented by a sentence, especially in hortatory genre. In the examples already discussed above, the complex cluster in Phlm. 13–14 is part of a long sentence. But, in the Col. 1:21–23, the whole paragraph is a single surface-structure sentence. The first cluster is represented by a clause in the Greek text, and the longer, final cluster, consisting of six propositions, is represented by the same number of clauses, which constitute the final part of the long sentence.

More significant, however, is the fact that the start of the surface representation of a propositional cluster in the New Testament Greek epistles is commonly indicated by certain conjunctions (*kai* 'and', *de* 'and, but', and *gar* 'for, since'), by asyndeton (i.e., lack of any conjunction), by the relative pronoun, and by an orienter (especially a performative). In a study of 120 propositional clusters in 2 Timothy and Hebrews, it was found that over 80% of the propositional clusters were initiated in one of the four ways listed above: *kai*, *de*, and *gar* accounted for 43%; asyndeton, 22%; relative pronouns, 11%; and orienters, 9%. (The other propositional clusters were initiated by other conjunctions, such as *oun* 'therefore' and *alla* 'on the contrary', or by participles.) It is important to note, however, that all of these initiating features also operate on higher levels than the propositional cluster. (There is also growing evidence that propositional clusters in narrative genre are most often introduced by *kai* and *de*.)

It is also very commonly the case that a finite verb is used to represent the Event concept in the head proposition of a propositional cluster. In the 87 propositional clusters studied in 2 Timothy, 77 of them had a finite verb representing the Event concept in the head proposition, i.e., 89%. It should be kept in mind, however, that the presence of a finite form of the verb does not always indicate a new cluster. In 2 Timothy, for example, there are 139 finite verbs of which only 77, approximately half, occur in main propositions.

Thus, typically, the surface representation of a propositional cluster in New Testament Greek will have a finite verb representing the central constituent of the head proposition and will begin in one of the four ways listed above.

7.8 Summary

The propositional cluster is a combination of propositions manifested in the surface structure as a clause, group of clauses, or a sentence. It has a proposition, or an Orienter with Content, as its head constituent, which is clarified, argued for, or added to by the other propositions.

The propositional cluster has referential and structural coherence, and it has features of natural and marked prominence. The prominent content of the propositional cluster consists of the head proposition(s), to which all the others are related by communication relations, together with any of the constituent propositions highlighted by marked prominence.

ANALYTICAL FEATURES	UNITY: Two or more constituents, one of which is a proposition and the others of which are propositions and/or other propositional clusters, combine to develop what is conceptualized as a single topic.	INTERNAL COHERENCE: Constituents which are compatible in the referential world, the communication situation, and the discourse structure are related in an appropriate manner using communication relations.	PROMINENCE: Natural relative prominence between the interrelated constituents isolates one or more head propositions from the other constituents that support it. Marked prominence may highlight one or more supporting constituents.
HOLISTIC FEATURES	CLASS: Based on the head proposition, it is a statement, command, or question pertaining to an event or state. (See discussion of proposition for sub-classification.)	EXTERNAL COHERENCE: As a compatible and appropriately related constituent of a paragraph (typically), it may serve either as the head or as a support unit, with any of the communication roles.	THEMATIC CONTENT: The central proposition with or without an orienter, plus any highlighted proposition(s), constitute the thematic content which contributes to the purpose of the unit of which it is a constituent.

Figure 7.8. The meaning features of the propositional cluster.

8

THE COMMUNICATION RELATIONS AND ROLES

8.1 Relations and roles distinguished

Every configuration of propositions consists of propositions related to one another by what are called the *communication relations*. Looked at from a different perspective, communication relations are those relations which relate propositions to each other in configurations. Thus, the communication relations are fundamental to the production of well-structured discourse and to its analysis. Without them, all discourses would consist of single propositions, unconnected with any other propositions. Further, the same set of relations is used regardless of whether it is two propositions that are being linked together, or two large units, such as divisions, parts, acts, etc. Because of the importance of these relations for any extended communication, they are described and discussed in some detail in this chapter.

Every propositional configuration can be viewed from two different perspectives. It can be examined from the point of view of its internal arrangements, or it can be viewed as a whole, i.e., as to what part it plays in the larger context in which it is found. The first of these perspectives is what gives rise to the analytical features, and it is from this perspective that *relations* are spoken of—they are what tie the various members of the unit to each other and to the central constituent. The second of these perspectives is what gives rise to the holistic features, and it is from this perspective that *roles* are spoken of. From the analytical perspective, the relations are "links" between the various parts that make up a unit. From the holistic perspective, the role is the "functional contribution" that a particular unit gives to the structure of which it is a constituent—whether it is a proposition in a cluster, a cluster in a paragraph, a paragraph in a section, etc.

The above statements define the sense in which the terms "relations" and "roles" are used in this theory. The discussion, however, may have given the impression that there is very little connection between the two. Such an impression would be misleading. Consider the two propositions (adapted from Col. 3:8):

(1) Do not act in an evil manner.
(2) Do not get angry in any way.

As a pair of propositions, related to each other in a propositional cluster, it can be seen that proposition 1 is more generic than proposition 2. "Acting in an evil manner" covers a wide variety of possible evil actions; "getting angry" is one particular sort of evil behavior. From the relational point of view, these two propositions are linked by what can be called a Generic-Specific relation, which is the relation which links together communication units where the content of one is generic relative to that of the other.

If we now ask what the role of proposition 1 is, the answer will be: it has a generic role. The part it plays in paragraph 3:5–11 of Colossians is to make a generic statement to which a number of specific statements are then related. So the same labels are used for both relations and roles. Most relations, however, are binary in name, since they link two communication units; roles are single in name because only one unit is being described as to its function.

One final general comment on relations and roles can be made. In the example cited, there was no explicit relator word in the surface structure—the relation and roles discussed were arrived at by a study of the content of the two propositions involved. Of course, there often is an explicit conjunction or preposition (New Testament Greek, in particular, uses conjunctions frequently), and if so, this will be carefully noted and studied in connection with the content of the unit under consideration. Both relations and roles are determined by studying all the relevant data—overt relator words, the presence or absence of finite forms of the verb, mood, the content of the units, etc. In the last analysis, however, it is the content of the units that is the most important, since relations and roles can be determined (as shown above) even when there are no overt relators. When surface-structure, relation-marking devices are used, it is the semantic content that ultimately defines the relation signaled by the surface-structure devices, and not vice versa.

8.2 Communication relations and discourse genre

In chapter 4, the four major discourse types of narration, exposition, exhortation, and procedure were distinguished, with two minor types, description and dialogue, also being recognized. Narrative and procedural discourse were distinguished from the other two major types on the basis of the chronological framework which is always present in these two types, and absent from the other two. Dialogue is also based on a chronological framework.

Genre distinctions are important for a study of communication relations, but a somewhat different classification is needed from that given in section 4.2. For communication relations, it is important to draw a distinction between *narrative* genre (including dialogue) and *nonnarrative* genres. The reason for this is that a whole class of relations which we refer to as *stimulus-response* relations is characteristic of narration (or even more strictly, of plot narrative; see section 4.2.4.b), and of dialogue. For the most part, such relations are not found in the other genres, except as narratives and dialogues are embedded in them. The converse, however, is not true. Narrative and dialogue readily make use of the relations found in the other genres, though generally only at the lowest level—i.e., within propositional clusters. Propositional clusters, paragraphs, episodes, etc., in narrative genre are typically related to each other by the various plot-structure, stimulus-response relations.

There is thus a broad division that can be made between relations that tend to be characteristic of narrative and those that tend to be characteristic of nonnarrative.

8.3 Generic classification of relations

In considering how to group the different kinds of relations which link semantic units together, we have found that there are several possible parameters which could be brought into play to categorize and subcategorize them:

1. Sequential versus simultaneous (Beekman 1970a)
2. Temporal versus logical (Hollenbach 1975)
3. Logical versus nonlogical
4. Causal versus noncausal
5. Chronological versus nonchronological
6. Situational versus referential (internal versus external, in Halliday and Hasan 1976) (pragmatic versus semantic, in Van Dijk 1977)
7. Narrative versus nonnarrative
8. Binary versus N-ary (Beekman and Callow 1974, Hollenbach 1975)
9. Addition versus support (Beekman and Callow 1974) (paratactic versus hypotactic versus neutral, in Grimes 1975) (coordinate versus subordinate, in Fuller 1969)
10. Symmetrical versus asymmetrical (Hollenbach 1973a)
11. Basic versus elaborative (Longacre 1980)
12. Etc.

The system presented here, and summarized in the chart at the end of the chapter, classifies the relations using a number of these and other parameters. The first distinction made in the system centers around the types of semantic units involved in the relationship. There are those communication units that serve to delimit the scope of a concept. That is, the proposition or propositional configuration is, in effect, functioning as a constituent of a concept, i.e., it is embedded. Strictly speaking, then, such constructions are not propositional configurations but are, in fact, concepts. They have been included in this discussion so that all of the relations that communication units are commonly involved in will be handled in a single location. Set off against this class is a large grouping of relations between communication units, the main concern of this paper.

The second major distinction in the system is between relations which link units of equal prominence and those which link units of unequal prominence. The name given to the former is *addition* relations.

Each of these two classes of relations is further subdivided by the parameter chronological-nonchronological. By "nonchronological" is meant that there is no focus on a temporal notion in the relationship. There may or may not be an implicit temporal relationship between the pair of communication units, but since it is not being highlighted in the relationship, the relationship is regarded a nonchronological.

There are yet further subdivisions among the relations that link units of unequal natural prominence. These will be treated as each of the subgroupings is dealt with in the discussion to follow. They are simply listed in figure 8.1, which displays the main groupings of relations between communication units.

The terms *addition* and *support*, rather than the corresponding grammatical terms, coordinate and subordinate, are used for relations between communication units to draw attention to the fact that these are *semantic* relations, not grammatical ones. It is true that, quite often, semantic units in an addition relation would be signaled in the surface structure by coordinate grammatical units, and that semantic units in a support relation would be signaled by a subordinate grammatical construction, but it is a fundamental tenet of this theory that skewing or mismatching can and does occur between surface structure and the semantic structure it represents. So, although there is the correlation mentioned above, it is also the case that a coordinate construction in the surface structure can represent a support-head relation, and a subordinate type of construction can represent one of the addition relations. The stimulus-response relations, which occur primarily in narration and, therefore, are based on a sequence of events in time, are generally represented by coordinate constructions in the surface structure. Such is the case even though these typically do not involve equal natural prominence.

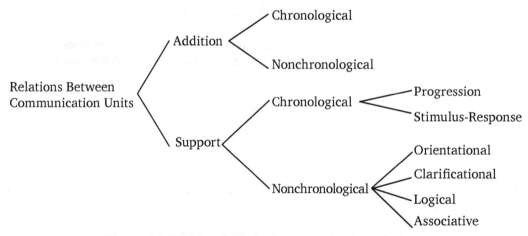

Figure 8.1. Main groupings of communication relations.

8.4 The chronological addition relations

The semantic component of chronology, or temporal focus, figures quite significantly into much of human communication. Languages will differ radically as to how they handle the chronological relationship between events. Barbara Hollenbach (1973a) has given an excellent presentation of some of the variables that affect how the temporal aspects of an event may be treated. She mentions such things as the following:

1. Duration of the events
2. Placement of the events with respect to a real-world time continuum
3. Number of the events
4. Frequency of the events
5. Phase of the events (i.e., beginning, middle, end).

Then, when events are considered in relation to one another, the temporal notions of succession and simultaneity come into play, yielding numerous possible chronological relationships. Again, Barbara Hollenbach (1973a) suggests the following:

1. Simultaneity (when events are of equal duration)
2. Span-included (when an event of short duration occurs during the span of an event of longer duration)
3. Semiantecedent-semisubsequent (when two spans have partial overlap)
4. Antecedent-subsequent (when one event precedes another, without overlap)
5. Beginning-postspan (when one event marks the beginning of another)
6. Prespan-end (when one event marks the end of another).

Robert Longacre (1980) subcategorizes temporal relations in a similar way. He lists four types of temporal overlap:

1. Span-span (when durative events are more or less coterminous)
2. Event-span (when a punctiliar event takes place while a durative event is in progress)
3. Span-event (when a durative event takes place while a punctiliar one takes place)
4. Event-event (the simultaneous occurrence of two punctiliar events).

Then he gives four varieties of succession:

1. Span-span (when two durative events follow one after another)
2. Event-span (when a punctiliar event is followed by a durative event)
3. Span-event (when a durative event is followed by a punctiliar event)
4. Event-event (when a punctiliar event is followed by another punctiliar event).

In the system of communication relations presented here, we have chosen to use the more generic labels, Sequential and Simultaneous. The specific subvarieties that one may use will be determined by language-specific needs.

8.4.1 Sequential

Since events involved in a Sequential relation are regarded as having equal natural prominence (i.e., addition relations), their roles, more specifically labeled, would be sequential $Head_1$, sequential $Head_2$, sequential $Head_n$. See figure 8.2.

8.4.2 Simultaneous

As was true with events related sequentially, the roles of events that are simultaneous will be simultaneous $Head_1$, simultaneous $Head_2$, simultaneous $Head_n$. See figure 8.3.

8.5 The nonchronological addition relations

8.5.1 Conjoining

One of the distinctions between the addition relations and the support relations is that the former are N-ary, the latter binary. More specifically, the particular addition relation of Conjoining is N-ary, that is to say, a unit can be conjoined to another unit which in turn can be conjoined to a third unit, and so on. Also, when it is said that a support relation is essentially binary, this does not mean that it is impossible for more than one support unit to be related to the same head unit at the same time. Figures 8.4 and 8.5 illustrate this. In figure 8.4, the two propositions are related by one of the support relations, Generic-Specific, with proposition 1 the more prominent of the two and thus labeled HEAD. But, in fact, Col. 3:8 has more than just one specific. The fuller picture is given in figure 8.5. There is still a binary, Generic-Specific relation between proposition 1 and each of propositions 2, 3, 4, 5, and 6. But propositions 2–6 are in a relation of Conjoining with each other. Conjoining, then, is a relation by means of which more than one unit can have the same relation to another unit.

Head units may also be related by Conjoining, as in the saying, "Let us eat, drink, and be merry, for tomorrow we die." Figure 8.6 shows this expression in a more proposition-like form and with the relations displayed diagrammatically. Here, proposition 4 is providing grounds for each of the three commands. In other words, propositions 1–3 are Conjoined, and proposition 4 is the supporting Grounds for the triple command.

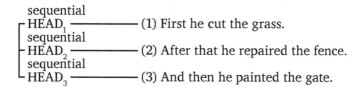

```
        sequential
   ┌ HEAD₁ ─────────── (1) First he cut the grass.
   │    sequential
   ├ HEAD₂ ─────────── (2) After that he repaired the fence.
   │    sequential
   └ HEAD₃ ─────────── (3) And then he painted the gate.
```

Figure 8.2. Sequential relation.

```
     simultaneous
   ┌ HEAD₁ ─────────── (1) Al cut the grass.
   │  simultaneous
   ├ HEAD₂ ─────────── (2) Meanwhile Bill repaired the fence.
   │  simultaneous
   └ HEAD₃ ─────────── (3) And at the same time Carl painted the gate.
```

Figure 8.3. Simultaneous relation.

```
   ┌ HEAD ─────── (1) Do not act in an evil manner.
   └ specific ─────── (2) Do not get angry in any way.
```

Figure 8.4. Simple binary relation.

```
   ┌ HEAD ─────────── (1) Do not act in an evil manner.
   ├ specific₁ ─────── (2) Do not get angry in any way.
   ├ specific₂ ─────── (3) Do not act maliciously.
   ├ specific₃ ─────── (4) Do not slander people.
   ├ specific₄ ─────── (5) Do not talk abusively to people.
   └ specific₅ ─────── (6) Do not tell lies to one another.
```

Figure 8.5. Conjoining and the binary relationships.

```
   ┌ HEAD₁ ─────────── (1) Let us eat
   ├ HEAD₂ ─────────── (2) and let us drink
   ├ HEAD₃ ─────────── (3) and let us be merry
   └ grounds ─────────── (4) for tomorrow we will die.
```

Figure 8.6. Conjoining of heads.

8.5.2 Alternation

The other addition relation is that of Alternation. Alternation may be either contrastive or supplementary (see figure 8.7). The contrastive form occurs in pairs which are antonyms, such as "dead" or "alive," or "present" or "absent" (see figure 8.8); or in pairs which are experiential opposites, such as "God" or "man"; or "by air" or "by sea" (see figure 8.9). Supplementary alternatives occur with a series of two or more choices all of which are in the same semantic domain (see figure 8.10).

Other examples of the types of Alternation are:

Matt. 6:31 "… 'What shall we eat?' or 'What shall we drink?' or 'What shall we wear?'…" (supplementary alternatives)

Matt. 11:3 "Are you the one who was to come, or should we expect someone else?" (experiential opposites: the two questions are essentially equivalent to saying: "Are you the one or are you not?")

1 Cor. 11:4 Every man who prays or prophesies with his head covered dishonors his head. (supplementary alternatives)

Jas. 2:3 …but say to the poor man, "You stand there" or "Sit on the floor by my feet." (experiential alternatives)

8.6 The chronological support relations: progression

Temporally-related events may be presented with equal natural prominence or with unequal natural prominence, i.e., they may be in an addition relation to one another or they may be in a support-head relation to one another. We have already discussed the chronological addition relations (section 8.4). There it was noted that temporally-related events may be sequential or simultaneous. These same two generic categories apply in support relations as well. The simultaneous events are handled by the orientation relations (see section 8.8). In such cases, the temporal component is downplayed so significantly that the relation is regarded as nonchronological. On the other hand, temporally-sequential events that are in a support-head relationship still have a high degree of focus on the temporal aspect; therefore, they are regarded as chronological.

There is a significant distinction among chronological support-head relations. Some involve a component of cause-effect, or stimulus-response, and another does not. Here we will deal with the one that does not have a stimulus-response feature, but rather has a notion of progression.

TYPE	POINT OF DIFFERENCE
Contrastive	antonyms
	experiential opposites
Supplementary	two or more choices within the same semantic domain

Figure 8.7. Alternation.

alternate
HEAD₁ ——————— (1) Is it lawful to pay a poll tax to Caesar
alternate
HEAD₂ ——————— (2) or (is it) not (lawful…)?

Figure 8.8. Mark 12:14—contrastive alternatives: antonyms.

alternate
HEAD₁ ——————— (1) Was the baptism of John from Heaven (God)
alternate
HEAD₂ ——————— (2) or (was it) from men?

Figure 8.9. Mark 11:30—contrastive alternatives: experiential opposites.

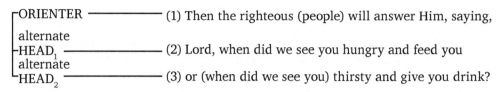

Figure 8.10. Matt. 25:37—supplementary alternatives.

When we say that events may be related by progression, while not involving a stimulus-response relationship, we mean that there is a necessary sequencing of the events—that is, $event_1$ must precede $event_2$, which must precede $event_3$, and so on. However, $event_1$ does not give rise to $event_2$, $event_2$ does not give rise to $event_3$, and so on. In a sequence of events of this nature, the last one is prominent and the others are considered to progressively lead up to it; therefore, they are labeled $step_n$-GOAL. An example of this relation is given in figure 8.11.

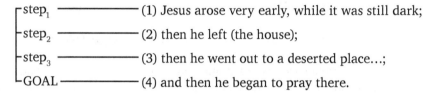

Figure 8.11. Mark 1:35—example of Step-Goal relation.

8.7 The chronological support relations: stimulus-response

As has already been pointed out, the stimulus-response relations are confined to narrative and dialogue units. They involve a focus on sequence in time, which distinguishes them, in general, from other support-head relations. Also, a distinction has been made between chronological support-head relations that involve a cause-effect component and another that does not. The latter has been described as involving progression and the former as involving stimulus response. In this regard it might be useful to note that the relation of progression, more specifically Step-Goal, always involves a single doer of the events; whereas in stimulus-response relations, the events so related will usually involve different doers, although not invariably. The key feature that characterizes the stimulus-response relations is that the stimulus event gives rise to or elicits the response event.

Stimulus-response relations are further subdivided into those involving speech and those that do not. We will first present and illustrate those that involve speech.

But first, one other interesting point must be made. One of the characteristics of dialogue and narrative is the flexibility with which the different stimuli and responses can occur together. This is a further distinction between them and the other support-head relations, where, for example, a Specific is always connected with a Generic and cannot be correlated with a Consequence, a Result, etc. Because of this flexibility, it is more convenient, when discussing stimulus-response relations, to focus on the role that a given unit has. Indeed, there are roles that frequently form a stimulus response pair, such as Question and Answer; but even so, a Question may be paired with a Counterquestion, an Evaluation, or even a Reaction. A Proposal will often be paired with an Execution, but certainly not invariably.

8.7.1 Speech stimulus and response roles

The speech roles are closely based on the three illocutionary functions of a proposition—statement, command, and question—and on their conventionally expected responses.

Remark is any type of statement that may be made, such as a rebuke, an accusation, a compliment, etc.

Counterremark is any statement that another speaker makes in connection with a prior Remark, and that does not express agreement or disagreement but makes an alternative or substitute Remark.

Proposal is any type of command, such as an exhortation, invitation, offer, plan, command, prohibition, suggestion, advice, counsel, directions, challenge, etc.

Counterproposal is a response to a Proposal which offers an alternative Proposal. It may, therefore, be any one of the specific types listed under Proposal. If the second speaker does not make a Counterproposal, he generally responds with an agreement or rejection of the original Proposal.

Question refers to any type of question, such as an interrogation on a witness stand, in contests, or in school; or any inquiry for direction or other information.

Counterquestion is a response to a Question with an alternative Question.

Answer is a response that is directly relevant to the inquiry made, even if it is: "I do not know." An example of the series Question-Counterquestion-Answer is given in figure 8.12.

Speaker 1:	How do I get to the shopping center?	(Question)
Speaker 2:	Why do you want to go there?	(Counterquestion)
Speaker 1:	To visit my uncle.	(Answer)

Figure 8.12. Example of Question-Counterquestion-Answer series.

Execution, strictly speaking, is not a speech role. However, it is included in this class since it is the natural counterpart of the Proposal, which is characteristically a speech role. It is an event or series of events which brings to pass what was proposed or planned. (The Proposal is most often given in the form of speech; however, the narrator may simply state that a proposal, plan, etc., was made.)

Evaluation is a statement made in connection with a prior speech stimulus; in it the speaker gives his assessment or interpretation of the speech element, e.g., he says it is good/bad, wise/foolish, thoughtful, helpful, inappropriate, etc. Figure 8.13 is an example of this role.

Speaker 1:	It is really hot today.	(Remark)
Speaker 2:	It was quite cool yesterday.	(Counterremark)
Speaker 1:	I really *love* cool weather.	(Counterremark)
Speaker 2:	You ought not to have such strong feelings about the weather.	(Evaluation)

Figure 8.13. Example of Evaluation.

Counterevaluation is a statement made in connection with a prior Evaluation, in which a speaker gives an alternative or substitute Evaluation for that already made. It should be noted that all "Counter–" roles are inherently reiterative. An Evaluation may be followed by a Counterevaluation, which, in its turn, may give rise to a further Counterevaluation. Similarly, a Proposal may give rise to any number of Counterproposals.

Reply is a verbal response to a Remark, Counterremark, Proposal, Counterproposal, Question, or Counterquestion, which is either one of acceptance or rejection. It may not be obvious from this definition how an acceptance of a Question would differ from an affirmative Answer to it. The two examples in figure 8.14 illustrate the difference between them. A further example of Reply is given in figure 8.15.

| Is this how you spell "occurrence"? | (Question) |
| Yes, it is. | (Answer) (affirmative) |

| Is this how you spell "occurrence"? | (Question) |
| Let me go look in Webster's. | (Reply) (acceptance) |

Figure 8.14. Comparison of an affirmative answer and an acceptance of a question.

Speaker 1:	Let's go to McDonald's for a hamburger.	(Proposal)
Speaker 2:	Let's go to Wendy's instead.	(Counterproposal)
Speaker 3:	That's a good idea.	(Reply)

Figure 8.15. Example of Reply.

Although very few examples of stimulus-response sequences involving speech have been given, theoretically almost any combination of these could occur. The potential options are such that it would be wearisome to attempt to describe the various possibilities. Perhaps one further example between only two speakers will suffice to illustrate the possibilities (see figure 8.16).

Speaker 1:	Where are you going, Bill?	(Question)
Speaker 2:	That's none of your business.	(Evaluation)
Speaker 1:	I can see you are in a bad mood today.	(Evaluation)
Speaker 2:	You have slim evidence to make such a comment.	(Evaluation)
Speaker 1:	What evidence should I have?	(Question)
Speaker 2:	Something more than my frankness in reminding you to mind your own business.	(Answer)

Figure 8.16. Combinations of speech stimulus and response roles.

Actual dialogues, of course, often do not consist of relatively short and simple speeches, and the same speaker may use two different roles in the same stretch of speech. The short conversation in figure 8.17 is adapted from *The Hobbit*, by J. R. R. Tolkien.

Gandalf:	"I will give you what you asked for."	(Reply (to an earlier Proposal))
Bilbo:	"I beg your pardon, I haven't asked for anything!"	(Evaluation (of Gandalf's Response, saying, in effect, it is erroneous))
Gandalf:	"Yes, you have. Twice now. My pardon...	(Evaluation)
	"In fact, I will go so far as to send you on this adventure."	(Remark)
Bilbo:	"Sorry! I don't want any adventures, thank you. Not today. Good morning!"	(Reply)
	"But please come to tea—any time you like...Come tomorrow! Good bye!"	(Proposal)

Figure 8.17. Complexity of speech stimulus and response roles in dialogue.

8.7.2 Nonspeech stimulus and response roles

Thus far in our research on narrative, the following list of roles has proven satisfactory. However, we present it with the awareness that further research may add to them or subtract from them, and may also modify the definitions that are given.

Occasion is an event or series of events which, even though it is weaker than an efficient cause, does set up the situation from which the following event(s) flow. That is, it has a stimulus role with respect to the following event(s). (In some analyses previously done, the labels "initiating incident" or "occasioning incident" have been used for the same role.)

Outcome is an event or sequence of events which comes about as a response to previous events. It is the natural counterpart of a previous Occasion. Outcome is not to be confused with Resolution. When they both occur, the Outcome will usually be a further response beyond that of the Resolution. The Resolution is the more direct response to a Problem; the Outcome would be a response to the whole story, i.e., to the Problem-Resolution pair, which constitutes the Occasion for the Outcome.

Problem is a generic label which is intended to include any type of "imbalance," such as a lack, threat, loss, disaster, tragedy, accident, crisis, need, etc. As was stated in chapter 4, the role of Problem is essential in all problem plot narratives. The Problem may be presented in the form of a Question, Remark, or Proposal. However, since the problem plot structure is so basic to the genre, we have chosen to give priority to the Problem-Resolution roles in the analysis. So, even though the Problem may be a Remark, it will be labeled "Problem." An alternative is to use dual labels, such as "Problem (Remark)."

Complication is an event or sequence of events which increases the Problem and moves it further away from a Resolution.

Resolving Incident is an event or sequence of events which moves toward a Resolution of a Problem or Complication, but does not fully resolve it.

Resolution consists of an event or sequence of events which resolves a Problem or a Complication. This generally involves a return to normalcy, i.e., when the imbalance has been stabilized, the need liquidated, etc. A Problem reaches its Resolution when it no longer exists. There will be situations in which the analyst might prefer the precision of such terms as Restoration, Restitution, Exoneration, or others, over the generic *Resolution*. Rather than to multiply the number of terms, the generic term *Resolution* has been selected to cover these ideas.

8.7.3 Stimulus-response structure illustrated

Two examples of narrative, with the plot structure identified, are given in figures 8.18 and 8.19. The propositional form used is not necessarily a final or polished one, as the main purpose is to illustrate the roles discussed above. Nor are any support-head roles within the units indicated. The structure is based on an analysis of Acts by Blood and Blood (1979). Both examples illustrate well how the member constituents can combine recursively to give larger groupings, which in turn relate to other such units in the overall structure. In example one, for instance, there are three main constituents, with the roles of Setting, Occasion, and Outcome, but the main Occasion is structurally complex.

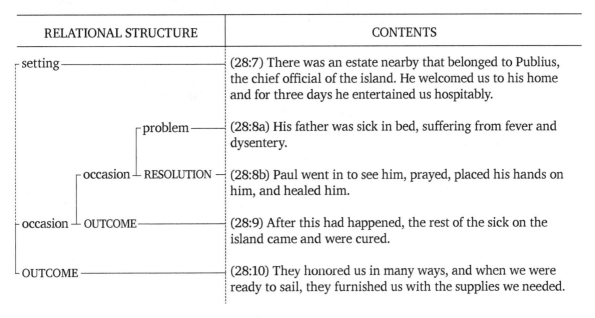

RELATIONAL STRUCTURE	CONTENTS
setting	(28:7) There was an estate nearby that belonged to Publius, the chief official of the island. He welcomed us to his home and for three days he entertained us hospitably.
problem	(28:8a) His father was sick in bed, suffering from fever and dysentery.
occasion — RESOLUTION	(28:8b) Paul went in to see him, prayed, placed his hands on him, and healed him.
occasion — OUTCOME	(28:9) After this had happened, the rest of the sick on the island came and were cured.
OUTCOME	(28:10) They honored us in many ways, and when we were ready to sail, they furnished us with the supplies we needed.

Figure 8.18. Acts 28:7–10.

RELATIONAL STRUCTURE	CONTENTS
setting	(3:1) Peter and John were going up to the temple at the hour (when people) prayed (publicly to God), (which was the ninth hour).
problem	(3:2) And a certain man was being brought (by people) to the temple. (This was a man who) was lame from the time when his mother bore him and whom (people) used to put each day at the temple gate (which people) called the beautiful (gate) (in order that he might) ask the people (who) entered the temple (that they) give him some money.
proposal	(3:3) He saw (that) Peter and John were about to enter the temple (and) he asked (them) (that he might receive some money from them).
COUNTERPROPOSAL	(3:4) Peter and John gazed at him (and) (Peter) said (to him): "Look at us!"
EXECUTION / occasion	(3:5) (So) he looked attentively at them (because) he expected (that he would) receive some (money) from them.
OUTCOME / proposal	(3:6) (Peter) said (to him): "(Although) I do not have any money, (yet) what I do have, this I give to you. By Jesus Christ, (who lived) in Nazareth, (now healing you), rise up and walk!"
occasion	(3:7a) And (Peter) grasped his right hand (and he) raised him up.
OUTCOME / occasion	(3:7b) And immediately (God) made his feet and ankles strong.
RESOLUTION / occasion — EXECUTION — OUTCOME	(3:8) And he leaped up (and) he stood and he was walking and he entered with them into the temple. (While he was entering,) he was walking (and) he was leaping (and) he was praising God.
occasion	(3:9) And all the people (there) saw (that he) was walking and (that he) was praising God.
OUTCOME / occasion	(3:10a) They recognized (that) this (man) was the person who sat at the gate of the temple in order that he might ask people that they give money to him.
OUTCOME — OUTCOME	(3:10b) And (all the people there) became greatly astonished and (they became) extremely bewildered (because) the man had become (well).

Figure 8.19. Acts 3:1–10.

Figure 8.19 illustrates how the stimulus-response roles frequently form *chains*. That is, a stimulus gives rise to a response which is itself a stimulus for a response, and so on. (S-R/S-R/S-R/S, etc.). Notice, for example, how the Resolution (3:3–8) consists of a stimulus-response chain: proposal-COUNTER-PROPOSAL *-EXECUTION/occasion-OUTCOME/proposal-EXECUTION. (*The "Counter" labels serve to indicate both the response role (Counter) and the stimulus role (Proposal).)

One point is not illustrated within these particular examples. As might be expected from the fact that the addition relations stand apart from the support-head distinction, the stimulus-response roles can be related by Conjoining. Thus, there could be two conjoined Occasions, two conjoined Outcomes, etc. Taking the episode of Acts 28:1–10 as a whole, however, paragraphs 28:1–6 and 28:7–10 are conjoined within the episode. Narrative, then, makes use of the relation of Conjoining at every level.

8.7.4 The primacy of stimulus-response roles over other types in narrative genre

In narration, there are times when it appears that either a stimulus-response or some other type of relation would appropriately represent the relation between a set of propositional configurations. For example, an Occasion may appear to represent an efficient cause, i.e., actually bringing about the events that follow. Thus, the relation could possibly be Reason. Although it is too early to become dogmatic concerning such instances, it would appear that the roles which are typical for a particular genre should be given preference and precedence over roles which are typical in some other genre. (See chapter 4 for the roles which are typically associated with the four major types of monologue.) Therefore, since the unit occurs in a narrative, and since narration is characterized by overt chronological sequencing, it stands to reason that the stimulus-response relations, which are chronological, would take precedence over the logical relations, which are nonchronological (i.e., time is not in focus).

8.8 The nonchronological support relations: orientation

The various nonchronological support-head relations are combined into four groups. The basis for doing this is the nature of the role of the supporting unit. When we ask: What is the supporting unit doing in relation to the head unit? the groupings that result are:

1. The *orientation* relations: the supporting unit orients the supported unit with respect to such matters as time, location, subject matter, etc.
2. The *clarification* relations: the supporting unit clarifies the supported unit by explaining it further or by restating it in some form.
3. The *logical* relations: the supporting unit argues for the supported unit by giving reasons, grounds, etc.
4. The *associative* relations: the supporting unit gives a nongermaine comment on the head unit or on some matter which was apparently suggested by its association with the head unit.

It follows from the above description that the less prominent unit is the one that orients, clarifies, argues, or is an associated comment; and the head unit is the one that is oriented, clarified, argued for, or commented on. Where there are exceptions or modifications to this general statement, they will be noted in connection with the particular relation concerned.

In the discussion that follows, we will first consider the *orientation* relations. Seven orientation relations are distinguished, although, as with many of the other support-head relations, some of these could be grouped together, or even finer distinctions could be made.

8.8.1 Circumstance/setting-head

As the support-head relations are binary in nature, each relation should, in theoretical precision, have a two-part label. Most do, but for some no convenient label has been found. In such cases, "Head," a neutral term, will be supplied.

In the relation of *Circumstance,* the support unit (usually a proposition or propositional cluster) provides information about the *Event(s)* or *State(s)* that form a background for the main-line information presented in the head unit. Here are some examples of the relation of Circumstances, the support element being italicized:

Phlm. 10: "...Onesimus, who became my son *while I was in chains.*"
Jude 9: "...the archangel Michael, *when he was disputing with the devil about the body of Moses,* did not dare..."

John 15:8: *"When he* (the Counselor) *comes,* he will convict the world..."
1 Cor. 13:11: *"When I was a child,* I talked like a child..."

   Setting is a narrative counterpart to Circumstance. It provides information on time, location, participants, and background Events or States. It often consists of State propositions, but it may also include movement from one location to another, thereby placing a participant "on stage" for the following unit(s). Longer Settings may also include a minor nonproblem narrative. For example, Mark 2:1–2 provides the Setting for the episode consisting of 2:1–12. It can be expressed in propositions as in figure 8.20. Note that within this Setting, there is a stimulus-response chain which has as its main Outcome (proposition 5) the entrance upon a state of affairs that forms the backdrop for the events that follow.

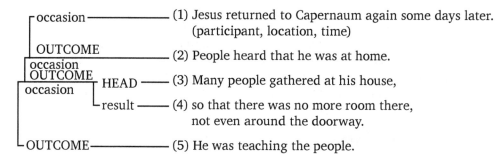

Figure 8.20. A setting with stimulus-response structure.

8.8.2 Time

The relation of Time is quite similar to that of Circumstance. Like Circumstance, Time provides background information for the main-line Events recorded in the head unit. As a matter of fact, a temporal component seems to be part of all of the Circumstance units as well. The Circumstance-Head relation appears to be saying that the head Event(s) took place during the time when the background Events or States were taking place. What distinguishes Time from Circumstance, then, is that Time does not involve Events or States other than those which communicate only a specific Time orientation, e.g., "after the sun went down...," "when several days had passed...," "when it was 3:45 in the afternoon...," etc.

8.8.3 Orienter-content

In this relation, a proposition or a propositional configuration introduces a unit which may range from a single proposition to a section, or even larger. The introducer proposition or configuration is called the Orienter; what it introduces is the Content. Five different types of Orienters are distinguished on the basis of the classification of the Event word(s) used in the Orienter proposition(s) (see figure 8.21). Examples are hardly necessary for this relation, but one is given below in which the Orienter is a propositional cluster rather than just a single proposition.

Type	Sample Event Words
SPEECH	said, commanded, warned, promised
PERCEPTUAL	saw, heard, felt, smelled, tasted
EMOTIONAL	rejoiced, thanked, prayed, wanted
COGNITIVE	knew, remembered, thought, agreed
VOLITIONAL	decided, willed, resolved, purposed

Figure 8.21. Types of Orienter.

Col. 1:9a *That is why we have also been praying constantly for you, since we heard the report about you, specifically, we have been asking God* that you will come to know fully... (This example is taken from the semantic-structure analysis of Colossians. There is a generic orienter ("praying") followed by a specific one ("asking"), together with a Circumstance proposition "since we heard the report about you.")

There are also two other types of content orienters which are not based on an Event concept in the Orienter proposition; in fact, they often occur in the form of State propositions. They are the *Evaluative Orienter* and the *Prominence Orienter*. The former is one that gives a value judgment on the content, e.g., "it is/is not good that...," "it is/is not true that," etc. The latter indicates that the content is to be given prominence, e.g., "this is important...," "pay attention to this...," etc. Strictly speaking, the Prominence Orienter could be considered a type of Evaluative Orienter, but it is treated separately because of the important part that the feature of prominence plays both in the theory and in analysis. Some examples of these Orienters are:

1 Cor. 7:1: "*It is good* for a man not to marry." (Evaluative Orienter)
1 Cor. 11:6: "...*it is a disgrace* for a woman to have her hair cut or shaved off." (Evaluative Orienter)
John 3:5: "*Amen, amen, I say to you,* unless a man is born of water and the Spirit..." (literal translation of the Orienter—a Prominence Orienter, equivalent to "What I am saying to you is important.")

Although it is convenient to recognize Evaluative and Prominence Orienters, and treat them as other Orienter-Content relations, strictly speaking, their Orienters plus their Content constitute a State proposition in which the topic takes the form of a proposition (or larger communication unit) and the comment is an Attribute (such as "good," "true," "important") related to the topic. Therefore, they are really a single State proposition with a communication unit functioning as topic, rather than two propositions related by a communication relation.

8.8.4 Opening-head; head-closing

When a whole discourse or a large relatively independent portion of one is considered, it is usually the case that it can be divided into three major parts. The labeling of these parts depends, very often, on the particular genre or subgenre. In general, there is some sort of "entrance" to the main body of the material, there is the main body itself, and not uncommonly there is some recognizable closure or ending. These are labeled "opening-HEAD-closing." (The Head may alternatively be labeled "BODY" and the closing "closure.") While it is true that the Body is more important than the other two parts and is, therefore labeled HEAD, it is possible that these major parts of the discourse are not strictly speaking support-head relations, but rather "part-whole" relations. However, since there are obvious parallels between these and the other orientation relations, they have been included here.

8.8.5 Introduction-head

The term Introduction is used only of information which introduces a communication unit of high level in the hierarchy—a section or larger unit. It is usually referred to as a *Prologue* when it occurs in narration. (See, for example, the analyses of Mark 1 by Larson (1979) and Kopesec (1978).) The Introduction may or may not include reference to the topic of the following units. For example, Col. 1:3–12 is analyzed as the Introduction to the Body of the Epistle. On the other hand, the introductory unit may only announce a topic, as in 1 Cor. 12:1, "Now about spiritual gifts, brother, I do not want you to be ignorant." "Spiritual gifts" is the topic of the next three chapters. In such cases, it is convenient to call this a *Topic Orienter*. If the Introduction includes some information on the thematic contents of the unit being introduced, rather than just its topic, it can be referred to as *Preview*.

8.8.6 Preliminary incident

Preliminary Incident is an event or sequence of events relevant to those that follow, but, like Setting, not entering into a stimulus-response relation with them. The difference between Setting and Preliminary

Incident is subtle. Even though a Setting may involve an "incident" (see figure 8.20), it functions to "set the stage" for the events of a narrative unit. It is concerned with what participants are involved in the events, when and where the events take place, and what was going on or what conditions prevailed at the time those events took place or began to take place. The Preliminary Incident, on the other hand, presupposes the Setting. It actually gets the events of the unit underway. But the events involved in it are not integral to the main stimulus-response structure of the unit. They involve some initial moves of the participant within the situation established by the Setting. In this sense, the Preliminary Incident could be thought of as a "secondary setting."

8.9 The nonchronological support relations: clarification

The clarification relations are divided into two subgroups on the basis of whether there is *overlap in content* between the two related units, or not. What is meant here by this is that the relation requires, by its very nature, that some significant part of the content of the two related units be the same. Trail (1973:21–22) describes this relationship as "…a conjunctive relationship in which one proposition repeats or restates, either verbally or conceptually, part or all of another…" There are thus two subgroups of the clarification relations, the "overlapping" and the "nonoverlapping" ones. The *overlapping clarification relations* will be treated first. They are Head-Equivalent, Head-Amplification, Generic-Specific, and Specific-Summary.

8.9.1 Head-equivalent

When two units which convey the same meaning are linked, the relation is Equivalence. This relation occurs in two forms. In the one, the same content is expressed by means of words or expressions which are synonymous in the particular context; this is referred to as *Equivalence by synonymous expression*. In the other, the content of the supporting proposition involves the negation of an antonym, so that this relation is labeled *Equivalence by negated antonym*. Equivalence often has the function of giving prominence by semantic repetition.

Some examples of Equivalence are given below. Some would fall into the classification of doublets, either of the synonymous or near-synonymous type:

Matt. 5:12 "Rejoice and be glad." (synonymous)
Matt. 5:17 "I have not come to abolish them but to fulfill them." ("Not to abolish" is equivalent to "fulfill" in this context, so this is an example of negated antonym.)
Matt. 6:24 "…Either he will hate the one and love the other, or he will be devoted to the one and despise the other." (In the context, "hate" and "despise" are regarded as near synonyms; similarly "love" and "be devoted to.")
Matt. 21:21 "If you have faith and do not doubt…" (negated antonym)
Rom. 9:1 "I speak the truth in Christ—I am not lying." (negated antonym)
Rom. 12:19 "'It is mine to avenge; I will repay,' says the Lord." (synonymous)

Probably translations of statements made in Aramaic should be included here. For example, Mark 5:41 (NIV) says, "…'*Talitha koum!*' (which means, 'Little girl…get up!')." The statements in the two languages are semantically equivalent.

Bruce Moore (1972) has provided an extensive and detailed analysis of doublets in the New Testament. He distinguishes between "synonymous" and "near-synonymous" doublets; the relation of Equivalence is used for both of these in the system of communication relations.

A question can be raised concerning the relative prominence of units related by Equivalence. When the two equivalent units are juxtaposed, as in all the above examples, then the second is considered to be supporting the first and of lesser prominence. However, if the two equivalent units are separated by some intervening support material, then they may be equally prominent. In hortatory genre, particularly, it seems to be the case that a command will be repeated (synonymously or near-synonymously) in a paragraph so that further supporting material may be attached to it. If all the supporting material were attached to the one initial command, the support would be very complex.

An example of this is found in Col. 3:1–4 ("set your hearts on things above" (3:1) and "set your minds on things above" (3:2)).

8.9.2 Head-amplification

This is a relation between two communication units in which one of the units communicates all of the information in the other, together with some further information. If the two units are propositions, then the added information in the Amplification proposition usually consists of concepts with such roles as Time, Location, or Manner. Where the units are larger, such as propositional clusters or paragraphs, then the added information is often propositions with a clarifying role. An example of this occurs in Col. 3:5–11. This paragraph consists of two complex propositional clusters. The second cluster has for its center a contracted form of the center of the first. The first (in 3:5) reads: "Do not act in an evil manner, like a dead person does not act in an evil manner." The second (in 3:8) reads, simply, "Do not act in an evil manner." Note that in the second the comparison with a dead person is left out. Both are followed by specific evil deeds to be avoided.

When the relation of Head-Amplification occurs between units larger than a proposition, it may well be an example of "packaging" in operation. For example, in the above analysis of Col. 3:5–11, Paul started with a general prohibition, and added five Specific prohibitions. Then, at 3:8, with the contracted form of the prohibition, he added another five Specific prohibitions, as well as two Grounds. It seems likely, then, that the "packaging" principle led him to avoid having a Generic prohibition followed by ten Specifics, as well as other information, such as Grounds. (Cf. a similar suggestion in connection with the relation of Equivalence above.)

When the units related by Head-Amplification are smaller units, such as propositions or propositional clusters, then the unit with the role of Amplification is regarded as prominent. At higher levels in the hierarchy, the contracted unit is the more prominent, the Amplification unit serving to clarify it.

8.9.3 Generic-specific; specific-summary

In this relation, the information communicated by the Head is generic in relation to that communicated by the support unit. The Generic unit, therefore, includes the information in the more Specific unit; so, in that sense, the Specific unit is repeating the information of the first unit, but it does so with a degree of detail which is only implied in the Generic one.

An example has already been cited of this relation from Col. 3:5–11, a hortatory paragraph (see figures 8.4 and 8.5). Other examples are:

Mark 6:48 "He went out to them [Generic], walking on the lake [Specific]."
Phlm. 20 "I do wish, brother, that I may have some benefit from you in the Lord [Generic]; refresh my heart in Christ [Specific]."

This is a relation that is frequently found between larger communication units. For example, Matt. 6:1–18 constitutes a section within the Sermon on the Mount. There are four constituents within it: 6:1, 6:2–4, 6:5–15, and 6:16–18. The last three constituents give three specific instances of the opening command "Be careful not to do your acts of righteousness before men," i.e., giving, praying, and fasting.

When a generic restatement of the content of some large unit (e.g., an act in narrative genre or a section in expository genre) *follows* the larger unit, then it is generally referred to as a *Summary*. Examples of these are found, for instance, at various points in the book of Acts. For example,

Acts 6:7 "So the word of God spread. The number of disciples in Jerusalem increased rapidly, and a large number of priests became obedient to the faith."

8.9.4 Head-comparison

Now we will examine the *nonoverlapping clarification relations*, which are Head-Comparison, Head-Illustration, Head-Example, Head-Manner, and Contrast-Head.

The relation of Comparison is based upon some point of similarity between two concepts—i.e., between two Things, two Attributes, or two Events. In addition to the point of similarity, the two units that are related by Comparison must be affirmative, and there must also be some point of difference between them. Except for metaphors, the Comparison is overtly signaled in surface structures by comparison relators; e.g., "as" or "like" in English, *hōs* 'as', *eoiken* 'it is like', and the phrase *kath' homoiotēta* 'according to the likeness of' in Greek.

The relation of Comparison can be expressed in various forms, such as:

comparison by degree	e.g.,	I am taller than he (is).
		I am the tallest of all.
		I am not as tall as he is.
relative comparison	e.g.,	I am tall (and) he is tall.
		I am tall, like he is tall.
absolute comparison	e.g.,	I am just as tall as he is.

It is one of the characteristics of the relation of Comparison in European languages that information in the clarificational supporting unit which is identical with that in the head unit is frequently ellipsed in the surface structure, giving the impression that only one unit—often a proposition—is involved. In the following examples, such information is supplied in parentheses and the Comparison proposition is italicized.

Matt. 12:13 "…(his hand was) just as sound *as the other (hand was sound)*…" (Here the two Attributes "sound" are being compared, and the comparison is based on the degree of soundness, which is that of equality here. These are both State propositions.)

Jas. 1:6 "…he who doubts is (unstable) *like a wave of the sea, blown and tossed by the wind, (is unstable)*…" (This is a simile in which two Thing concepts, "he who doubts" and "a wave that is blown and tossed about," are compared. Again, the two propositions concerned are State propositions.)

2 Tim. 2:3 "Endure hardship (well)…*like a good soldier of Jesus Christ (endures hardship well)*." (This is also a simile in which the person addressed, Timothy, is compared to "a good soldier of Jesus Christ"—again two Thing concepts. The point of similarity, however, is an Event in this case, "endure hardship," not Attributes as in the two previous examples. The propositions are, therefore, Event propositions.)

8.9.5 Head-illustration

If the Comparison role is filled by a larger unit, such as a paragraph, then it is said to have the role of *Illustration*. This role is exemplified by the many parables that Jesus told, which start "The kingdom of heaven is like…" In a semantic analysis, a parable has a theme based upon an image such as a mustard plant (Mark 4:30–32), and from that theme (e.g., a mustard plant grows to be very large, starting from a very small beginning), the point of similarity (large growth from a small start) is found. When this point of similarity is collocated with the original topic of "the kingdom of heaven," the theme statement is arrived at. Thus, using the above example, and without using a strict representation of the propositions involved, the Comparison is as follows:

God will begin to rule over very few people and will eventually rule over very many people *just like the mustard plant starts as a very small seed and grows to be a tree.*

But in Mark 4:31b–32 the author expands the Comparison unit considerably. Consequently, the parable is said to have the role of Illustration rather than Comparison.

Illustrations do not have to be parables. The examples of live metaphors given in *Translating the Word of God* (Beekman and Callow 1974:133–134) would also be Illustrations. For instance, Mark 2:21–22, where Jesus used the series of interrelated images of an old garment, a new piece of cloth, sewing, and tearing, or Paul's comparison of the Church with a body in 1 Cor. 12:12–27, would have the role of Illustration.

8.9.6 Head-manner

The status of Manner as a valid communication role is somewhat tenuous. Callow (1977:23) writes: "The status and definition of the semantic relation of MANNER has been under constant discussion as problematical." Some classify it as part of the Case system (Longacre for one, 1980:212); others see it as an integral component of the event concept; still others give it full propositional status and regard it as related to another Event proposition. The two latter approaches are taken in the system of communication relations presented here. The following criteria are being used to distinguish the two:

1. If the unit is more precisely descriptive of the action itself, then it is regarded as a delimitational component of the Event concept. For example:

    "Jack ran *quickly* down the hill."

2. If the unit is more precisely descriptive of the one doing the action of the Event concept, then the modifier is regarded as a separate communication unit with the role of Manner. For example, the sentence, "Jill *frantically* tried to warn Jack about the stump" would be analyzed as a propositional configuration with a Head-Manner relation (see figure 8.22).

> ┌ HEAD ——————— (1) Jill tried to warn Jack about the stump.
> └ manner ————— (2) (While doing this) she was frantic.

Figure 8.22. Head-Manner configuration.

A Manner proposition, then, describes the state of the one(s) doing the action of the Head proposition.

Manner has traditionally been understood as describing "how" an Event was carried out; however, this definition has proven to be ambiguous. Figure 8.23 shows some of the features that distinguish Manner from some other roles that in one sense or another answer the "how" question. (See also Beekman and Callow 1974:293–294.)

CONTRASTIVE FEATURES				SUPPORT ROLE
CAUSAL (State/Event)				MEANS
NONCASUAL	SAME MAIN PARTICIPANT**	STATE		MANNER*
		EVENT	REPEATED COMPONENTS	SPECIFIC
			NO REPEATED COMPONENTS	CIRCUMSTANCE
	DIFFERENT MAIN PARTICIPANT**	(State/Event)		

* The HEAD (supported) proposition must be an Event.
** Same or different from the main participant of the HEAD proposition.

Figure 8.23. Manner compared with other "how" roles.

The notion of manner is sometimes carried by units having other basic communication roles:

1.   *Comparison* units often define the manner of an Event. For example:

    "John worked like a beaver." (i.e., diligently)

2.   *Result* units may define the manner of an Event, as in

    "He worked admirably." (This is equivalent to: "He worked (in such a way (implied manner)) so that others admired him.")

The close association of Manner, Comparison, and Result is seen in Greek and English surface structure (Figure 8.24).

	MANNER	COMPARISON	RESULT
GREEK	-ōs	hōs	hōste
ENGLISH	-ly (like), so	like, as	so that

Figure 8.24. The similarity of surface representation of Manner, Comparison, and Result.

8.9.7 Contrast-head

The relation of Contrast occurs between two communication units when there are at least two points of difference between them and one point of similarity. One of the points of difference involves an opposition. The opposition may be expressed in several different ways (figure 8.25). (In these examples from English, information that is normally ellipsed in the surface structure is provided in parentheses.)

1.   *Simple negation.* If the propositions are Event propositions, then in one the Event is affirmed, in the other it is denied; e.g., "I went to classes today, but Bill didn't (go to classes today)." If the propositions are State propositions, then the central concept is affirmed in one, denied in the other; e.g., "John is tall, but Bill is not (tall)."
2.   *Negation by exception.* This is perhaps a subvariety of group 1. In "Everyone went to the party, except Bill," the phrase "except Bill" is equivalent to "Bill did not go to the party"; so the central Event is denied. In such examples, it should be borne in mind that "everyone," strictly speaking, means "everyone minus Bill."
3.   *Negation of synonym.* Both propositions refer to the same Event, but use synonymous lexical items to do so, and in one of the propositions, the Event concept is negated, e.g., "Bill won the race yesterday, but John did not come in first (in the race yesterday)"; "John is greedy, but Bill is not a glutton."
4.   *Lexical antonyms.* The opposition is carried by a pair of lexical antonyms; e.g., "He stayed behind, but I departed"; "He is tall, but I am short." The relation of Equivalence (see section 8.9.1) can also occur in a form where an antonym is used. Consider, for example Matt. 5:17, one of the examples quoted in the section on Equivalence: "I have come not to abolish them, but to fulfill them." The opposition, which is expressed by the antonyms "abolish" and "fulfill" and by the use of "but," give a first impression that there is a relation of Contrast between the two halves of this statement. But this is an example of Equivalence, since, in this context "not abolish" is equivalent to "fulfill." So the same thing is being said in both halves. A good quick test is to insert "that is" or "which is the same as saying" between the two related statements and see if the whole still makes sense. If it does, then it is Equivalence; if not, then it is probably Contrast.

TYPE OF OPPOSITION	EXAMPLES		
	1st Difference	Difference by Opposition	Likeness
SIMPLE NEGATION	but Jack Jill	liked didn't (like	hiking, hiking).
NEGATION BY EXCEPTION	except Everyone Jill	liked (didn't like	Jack Jack).
NEGATION OF A SYNONYM	but Jill Jack	was astute, was not very intelligent.	[mental agility]
ANTONYM	but Jill Jack	was agile, was clumsy.	[physical adeptness]
DIFFERENCE OF DEGREE	but Jill Jack	walked fast, walked faster.	[rate of walking]
PREFERENCE	but Jack Jill	likes prefers	hot dogs, hamburgers. [food]

Figure 8.25. Types of opposition in Contrast.

5. *Difference of degree.* This form of Contrast is very similar to a Comparison. An example of Comparison by degree was given above: "I am not as tall as he is." This might be considered a form of Contrast since "I am short but he is tall," which is a form of Contrast using an antonym, or "I am tall but he is taller" could be semantically equivalent to "I am not as tall as he is." However, when the author chooses to say "I am not as tall as he is," he is focusing on a comparison (with regard to height) and chooses to express it using a negation. But the comparison is the primary focus. When he chooses to say "I am short, but he is tall," there is still a comparison with regard to height, but it is implicit, and the author chooses to present a contrast using antonyms. Thus, there is a close similarity between Comparison expressed negatively, Contrast by antonym, where the antonyms are Attributes on a continuum, and Contrast by degree; and it is primarily a matter of focus on the part of the author as to which form he chooses to communicate what he wishes to say.

6. *Preference.* In the first half of this pair, an Event is affirmed which in the second is implicitly negated by the expression of a preferred alternative. In "He stayed behind, but I preferred to leave," the second half implies the contrast "but I did not stay behind" or "but I left."

The similarity of Contrast to some of the other relations has led some to conclude that Contrast is not a separate relation but rather a modification of those other relations. This is certainly worthy of consideration.

8.10 The nonchronological support relations: logical

The third group of nonchronological support-head relations are labeled *logical* relations, since the notion of logical implication (cause-effect) is involved in them. Furthermore, since frequently the effect temporally follows the cause, some logical relations have an implicit chronological component. This time element, however, does not usually come to overt expression in these relations, unlike the stimulus-response ones, which always occur in the context of a time framework. Thus, the logical relations are regarded as nonchronological.

8.10.1 Reason-result; means-result; and means-purpose

It is convenient to discuss the first three relations in this set as a group since they are so closely interrelated. The differences between them are charted in figure 8.26.

Cause Effect	Cause with intention	Effect stated as:	Cause answers the question:
REASON-RESULT	no	realized	*Why* this result?
MEANS -RESULT			*How* did this result come about?
MEANS -PURPOSE	yes	intended	*What* action was undertaken to achieve the intended result?

Figure 8.26. Reason-Result, Means-Result, and Means-Purpose relations compared.

The component of *intention,* related to the cause, needs some further explanation. The usual way in which the relation of Means-Result is shown in English surface structure is with the use of "by" and the "-ing" form of the verb, as in "He kept fit *by jogging* three miles every day." But this surface-structure pattern encodes functions other than the Means-Result relation. So, before a proposition can definitely be classed as a Means, the element of intention or voluntariness must be present. Compare the two statements:

> He fell ill by studying twenty hours a day.
> He passed the exam by studying twenty hours a day.

In the first example, "he fell ill" was not (presumably) the intended result of such arduous study, so the "by" proposition would be analyzed as a Reason. In the second example, "he passed the exam" was (presumably) the intended result, so the "by" proposition would be analyzed as having the role of Means. Means, then, always carries this component of voluntariness or intention.

The intention or desire associated with the Means-Result relation can be made explicit. Compare the following two examples:

> He studied twenty hours a day in order to pass the exam.
> He wished to pass the exam; therefore he studied twenty hours a day.

In the second example, the desire has been made explicit in the communication. There is now a Reason-Result pairing, and the Reason consists of the orienter "he wished" and its content "to pass the exam." The first form, however, is common in languages and evidently is a widespread way of representing an intended or desired result, without overtly referring to the desire.

Several further observations can be made concerning these relations:

1. They can be presented in either order in the surface structure; i.e., the cause may be given first, or the effect.
2. Either side of the relation may have further units conjoined to it; e.g., a Result may be related to several Reasons, or a Reason to several Results.
3. The naturally prominent unit in the Reason-Result and Means-Result relations is the Result unit. In the Means-Purpose relation, however, it is the Means.

Here are some examples from the New Testament:

Matt. 8:24 "…a furious storm came up on the lake, so that the waves swept over the boat." (Reason-Result)
Mark 7:9 "You have a fine way of setting aside the commands of God in order to observe your own traditions!" (Means-Purpose)
Col. 1:22 "But now he has reconciled you…through death." (Result-Means)

A particular type of Means-Purpose merits special discussion. In the case where the Means is an Orienter together with a generic Content, such as "he said this" or "I have written this," the deictic pronoun "this" is a surface structure device to relate a Purpose to a higher-level communication unit. Such expressions as "this" or "these things" refer back to some higher-level unit, which may even be the discourse itself. The level of the unit to which the deictic refers indicates the level of the Purpose that is stated for it.

8.10.2 Condition-consequence

The three remaining relations are those of Condition-Consequence, Concession-Contraexpectation, and Head-Grounds. The cause-effect connection can still be posited as underlying these relations, but what is made prominent are the other factors that the author wishes to draw attention to. The general description of these three relations as cause-effect is based on the fact that the cause-effect notion is required in their explanation. What it does not mean is that the two elements of each relation are in a simple, direct, cause-effect relation. In the description of each of these three, further discussion is given to this matter as necessary.

The Condition-Consequence relation consists basically of two types (see also Barnwell 1980:184–186):

1. The Condition is known or assumed not to be the case, or not to have happened, and the speaker gives a hypothetical Consequence.
2. The Condition is uncertain, so far as the speaker is concerned, as to whether it took place, is taking place, or will do so.

So, in this relation there is always a hypothetical component present, or else one of uncertainty.

The first type is commonly known as a *contrary-to-fact* (or *contrafactual*) *condition*. The condition is known not to have taken place, or it is assumed that it did not. The assumption may, of course, be wrong, but that does not affect the relation. The same is true of the assumed consequence; that assumption, too, may be right or wrong.

Mark 14:21 "It would be better for him if he had not been born." (reverse order of Consequence-Condition)

Luke 7:39 "If this man were a prophet, he would know who is touching him..." (The Condition is a State proposition, which is assumed to be false; in the context, it proved to be a wrong assumption.)

The second type is known as a *potential-fact condition*, and it is subcategorized into *general* conditions, which can refer to any number of particular cases, and *particular* conditions, which refer to only one situation.

Matt. 8:2 "Lord, if you are willing, you can make me clean." (particular)

Matt. 14:28 "Lord, if it's you...tell me to come to you on the water." (particular; the Consequence is a command)

Matt. 15:14 "If a blind man leads a blind man, both will fall into a pit." (general)

John 3:3 "...unless a man is born again, he cannot see the kingdom of God." (general; both the Condition and the Consequence are negative (unless = if not))

2 Tim. 2:5 "...he does not receive the crown, unless he competes according to the rules." (general; the Consequence is stated first and both the Condition and Consequence are negative)

It has been rightly pointed out by Barnwell (1980:183–184) that the Condition-Consequence relation is always in combination with one of the other logical relations, resulting in a dual role for each proposition. But regardless of what the other relation is, when the author casts a cause-effect relation in the Condition-Consequence form, he apparently wishes to draw attention to the factors of uncertainty and hypotheticality rather than to the other underlying relation. So our present approach in labeling such relations is to give precedence to Condition-Consequence.

8.10.3 Concession-contraexpectation

This relation is characterized by a component of "unexpectedness." (Longacre (1976:149ff) refers to this as "frustration.") There are essentially three parts to a Concession-Contraexpectation: there is a cause, there is an expected effect, and there is an unexpected Event or State. Most often only two of the three parts will be overtly presented: the cause and either a denial of the expected effect, or the unexpected Event or State. Note the following examples:

(A) Although the doctor told Bill to stay at home, he went to a baseball game.
(B) The doctor told Bill to stay at home, but he didn't.
(C) In spite of the doctor's instructions, Bill went to a baseball game instead of staying at home.

In example A, the expected result of staying at home is not explicitly negated, but is implied by the explicitly stated, but unexpected, Event "he went to a baseball game." In B, the expected result is denied, but what actually happened is not stated. In example C, both are given.

Within a given speech community, what is expected and what is not expected to result from a particular cause, is commonly known. But in another community, the expectations may be quite different. So, when it comes to interpreting particular examples in the Scriptures, which reflect the expectations of a culture of 2000 years ago, it can be very difficult to decide whether an unexpected effect has indeed been stated. An example of this problem is found in Phlm. 11. A fairly literal translation of the Greek is "who formerly (was) useless to you, but now (has become) useful both to you and to me." Is this a Contraexpectation? In other words, was it unexpected in the culture of that time, that a runaway slave, who had probably stolen from his master, and whom Paul can describe as useless at that time, could ever be useful again? It is hard to say, but it seems likely that the answer would be yes, in which case the relation between these two statements would be Concession-Contraexpectation. This could be made clear by translating the sentence, "Although he was useless to you formerly, now he is useful both to you and me."

This example also shows the similarity between Contrast and Contraexpectation. If this is not interpreted as a Contraexpectation, then it becomes an example of Contrast, in which the opposition is expressed by means of the antonyms "useless" and "useful." It is the element of unexpectedness that distinguishes the relation of Concession-Contraexpectation.

Two Concession-Contraexpectation examples from Colossians are given below:

1:21 "Although you were formerly alienated from God and although you were formerly hostile to God, he has now reconciled you."
2:23 "...such rules only cause people to do what their evil nature wants to do, even though these rules seem to be wise." (Contraexpectation first)

Several rather complex forms of Concession-Contraexpectation require some further discussion.
1. Concession-Contraexpectation combined with Condition-Consequence. Here the cause on which the expected effect is based is expressed as uncertain; e.g., Matt. 26:35 "Even if I have to die with you, I will never disown you." Whether Peter was to die or not was uncertain, so there is a conditional factor present. But, there is also the general expectation that, faced with a choice between dying and disowning someone, the choice would be to disown the person concerned. Hence, there is the unexpectedness of preferring death to disowning Jesus. So, in terms of relations, it would be more specifically analyzed as Condition + Concession—Consequence + Contraexpectation.
2. Concession-Contraexpectation combined with proportion. Consider, for example, Mark 7:36: "The more he did so, the more they kept talking about it." In the context, "he did so" means "he commanded them not to tell anyone." In most (perhaps all) cultures, a command is expected to be obeyed, so their disobedience is contrary to expectation. But, in addition, the two Events are compared with each other, so that an increase in one corresponds with an increase in the other.
3. Concession-Contraexpectation with the Contraexpectation only implied. Consider the English example "I was going to go to the store, but it rained." It is not explicitly stated "I didn't go," but, in the context, it is clearly implied. Also, if there was the intention of going to the store, it would be a normal expectation that the person concerned would go. So there is a Concession-Contraexpectation relation, but the negation of the expected result is implied by a stated Reason of which it is understood to be the Result. A possible example of this from the New Testament could be 1 Thess. 2:18 "We wanted to come to you...but Satan stopped us." It is clearly implied that he had not gone to visit

them, because he was hindered by Satan. His desiring to go carries with it the expectation that he would do so. In fuller propositional form, it would be:

(1) We wanted to come to you.
(2) We didn't come to you
(3) because Satan stopped us.

So the basic question is how statements 1 and 2 are to be related, and the best analysis seems to be that of Concession-Contraexpectation. Thus, although only propositions 1 and 3 are represented in the surface structure, the implied proposition 2 indicates that the best analysis is one of Concession-Contraexpectation.

8.10.4 Head-Grounds

In this relation, a State or Event is stated (i.e., affirmed or denied), commanded, or questioned in the Head unit; and, in the Grounds unit, an observation or a known fact is given as the basis for doing so. Particularly important in this definition is that the Grounds supports not the State or Event

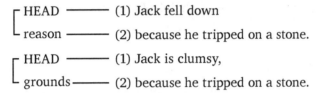

Figure 8.27. Reason versus Grounds.

(i.e., the referential aspect of the Head proposition), but the illocutionary act of stating, commanding, or questioning by the author (i.e., the situational aspect of the proposition). It is on this basis that Grounds can be distinguished from Reason. A Reason unit provides the basis for the referential aspects of the Head proposition. The two examples in figure 8.27 illustrate this quite clearly. In the second example the Grounds unit is not the cause of Jack being clumsy, but rather it is evidence for the *claim* that Jack is clumsy. Most likely the conjunction "because" would be omitted in natural English surface structure.

Three different types of Grounds have been distinguished:

1. *Evidential* Grounds, in which an effect is given as the basis for asserting the cause which gave rise to it; e.g., "It's cold outside; the river is frozen over." (The Head can be made more obviously a conclusion or deduction by saying "It must be cold outside; the river is frozen over.")
2. *Exemplary (historical)* Grounds, in which the Grounds is given in the form of an example, often a historical one; e.g., "You should wear gloves; look how George got his fingers frostbitten."
3. *Generic* Grounds, in which a specific conclusion is drawn from generic Grounds; e.g., "I am an apostle to the Gentiles, so I am an apostle to you," where "you" is understood to be Gentiles.

Some New Testament examples are given below:

Rom. 9:15–16 "I will have mercy on whom I have mercy, and I will have compassion on whom I have compassion. It does not, therefore, depend on man's effort, but on God's mercy." (This is a complex example in which there are two Conjoined Grounds (Old Testament quotations in this case), with two contrastive Heads.)

Heb. 4:14 "...since we have a great high priest...let us hold firmly to the faith." (Grounds-Exhortation)

1 Pet. 5:8 "Be self-controlled and alert. Your enemy the devil prowls around...looking for someone to devour." (reverse order of Exhortation-Grounds, with two Conjoined-Exhortations)

In connection with New Testament examples, it is worth pointing out that the Grounds for an Exhortation may be considerably developed. Col. 2:8–15 is essentially a paragraph consisting of an Exhortation (2:8) followed by three Conjoined Grounds. The first of these (2:9) is a proposition, but the other two (2:10–12 and 2:13–15) are complex propositional clusters.

8.11 The nonchronological support relations: associative

A growing number of situations have been encountered of units that depart from the main stream of the discourse, comment briefly on some point, and then return again to the mainline of discussion. It is usually quite clear what triggered the digression, since there is a fairly obvious informational link between the two units involved. However, the relation is none of the ones that have been treated thus far, whether addition or support-head. The relation is "accidental," or incidental, as opposed to the more integral ones that have already been treated. Such cases are assigned one of the associative relations—Comment or Parenthesis.

Comment is used to label associative units that more closely overlap with the subject matter of the unit of which it is a constituent. *Parenthesis* is used for those associative units that are quite peripheral to the discussion in progress at the time of the insertion.

A very clear example of Comment occurs in 2 Tim. 4:14–15 (figure 8.28). Propositional cluster 4:14b, "the Lord will punish him for what he did," arises out of Paul's mention of Alexander wronging him (4:14a). However, it is quite aside from the theme of the paragraph and does not support his point in any clear-cut way. Yet, there is a close enough link of the content of 4:14b with that of the rest of the paragraph that it is regarded as a Comment.

RELATIONAL STRUCTURE	CONTENTS AND LEVELS OF THEMATICITY
┌grounds ──┬─ HEAD ───────	(4:14a) Alexander, the man who makes things from copper, wronged me very much—
│ └─ comment ────	(4:14b) the Lord will punish him for what he did.
├HEAD ───────────────────	(4:15a) (Because he wronged me,) you yourself, too, must be alert (so that) he (will not wrong you).
└grounds ────────────────	(4:15b) (He will do it if he can,) because he very much opposes the message which we (preach).

Figure 8.28. 2 Tim. 4:14–15—Illustration of Comment.

A good illustration of Parenthesis is provided in 2 Tim. 4:19-22 (figure 8.29). It is not difficult to see how the two Parenthesis units (4:20 and 21a) would arise out of the content of the paragraph. Paul is mentioning various people known both to himself and Timothy and this causes him to think of Erastus and Trophimus whom he failed to mention earlier in paragraph 4:9–13, where 4:20 and 21a would have been most appropriate. But note that 4:20 and 21a are very peripheral to the rest of paragraph 4:19–22. They would fit very nicely into paragraph 4:9–13, but not so here; so they are labeled "parenthesis."

RELATIONAL STRUCTURE	CONTENTS AND LEVELS OF THEMATICITY
┌HEAD$_1$ ───────────────	(4:19) Greet (for me) Pricilla and Aquila and the family of Onesiphorus.
│ ┌parenthesis$_1$ ──	(4:20) Erastus stayed in (the city of) Corinth. Trophimus, I left in (the city of) Miletus because he was sick.
│ └parenthesis$_2$ ──	(4:21) Do your best to come to me before the stormy season.
├HEAD$_2$ ───────────────	(4:21b) Eubulus, Pudens, Linus, Claudia and many other fellow Christians greet you.
└HEAD$_3$ ───────────────	(4:22 (May) the Lord (help you in) your spirit, (Timothy and may he) bless (all of) you (Christians).

Figure 8.29. 2 Tim. 4:19–22—Illustration of Parenthesis.

8.12 Relations between communication units and concepts

This chapter has described the relations which exist between any and all communication units—propositions, propositional clusters, paragraphs, episodes, etc. To complete the picture, the reader is reminded that propositions (and, more rarely, larger communication units) can modify a *concept*. In such cases they function with one of the two delimitational roles of *Description* or *Identification*. Thus, in terms of a comprehensive review of all the roles that a proposition may have, Description and Identification are briefly mentioned here.

The purpose of a delimitational communication unit is to enlarge upon or give added specification to a concept of another communication unit. Such units are frequently represented in English surface structure (and in Greek) as relative clauses. Other representations are: adjectives, participles, prepositional phrases, independent clauses or sentences, etc. (e.g., "beloved," "coming," "with a headache," "I had an old car; it was two-toned blue.").

However, not all adjectival phrases or relative clauses are delimitational (e.g., compare Eph. 1:3 in NASB, Phillips, and TEV). It is important to ask what role the contents of such a unit might be playing in the development of the unit of which it is a constituent. Often logical points are subtly made by use of relative clauses, adjectival phrases, and participles.

IDENTIFICATION	DESCRIPTION
Semantic equivalent to a restrictive relative clause	Semantic equivalent to a nonrestrictive relative clause
Distinguishes one item from other similar items	Gives information about an item
Specifies contextually new information	Comments on contextually old information
Essential to the sense of the Head unit	Background with respect to the Head unit

Figure 8.30. Comparison of Identification and Description.

Figure 8.30 presents some of the features that distinguish Identification and Description. Barnwell (1980:208) has given an especially clear illustration of the difference between the two:

(1) The boys *who knew they were trespassing* [Identification] ran off quickly, leaving the others to face the farmer.
(2) The boys, *who knew they were trespassing* [Description], ran off quickly.

8.13 Prominence and the communication relations

8.13.1 Natural prominence

So far in this chapter, two basic statements have been made about prominence:

1. In addition relations, the units related are of *equal* prominence.
2. In support-head relations, the two units related are of *unequal* prominence.

In both of these cases, what is referred to is *natural* prominence—it is carried by the relationship as such. The question can be asked: What is the basis for considering this prominence to be natural, for saying that in support-head relations one of the units by nature carries more significance in the discourse than the other does?

In connection with this question, an experiment was carried out. Sixteen different colleagues, some of whom are linguists, some of whom are not, were asked a series of questions to determine which member of a pair they considered to be naturally prominent. The first question asked, "Which is more naturally prominent of these two colors, red or green?" was consistently answered by all that red is the more prominent. This was followed with a series of similar questions, each person being asked independently of the others to choose the prominent member in the following pairs: reason or result, conclusion or grounds, exhortation or motivation, stimulus or response, remark or evaluation, question or answer, command or its execution, an activity or its outcome. In all but two instances, the result (i.e., supported) unit and the response unit were selected as the more prominent, even though in framing some of the questions the order of the pair had been reversed. Two individuals chose the remark as being more prominent than the evaluation. In all other instances, the answers focused with little or no hesitation on the response or result half of each pair.

This experiment points to the conclusions that Linda Jones (1977:2–3) has expressed:

> Theme, I believe, is basic to being human. When we do something we thereby do not do something else: one thing is important, the other is less important. We consciously or unconsciously assign importance to certain actions in our lives, and less importance to others…Theme is thus deeply rooted in our very perception of the world around us. The human mind is incapable of assigning equal importance to all the data it receives from its sensory sources, probably because it is incapable of paying equal attention to all the data at once. When we look at a picture, we never perceive all its details simultaneously. There are certain parts of the picture that we notice immediately, while the rest we do not. Always in human perception there are foreground and background, figure against ground, important and not important, theme and not-theme (or background).

Thus, natural prominence in discourse is understood as one way in which the human mind expresses its inbuilt practice of assigning importance to one thing relative to another.

8.13.2 Marked prominence

Thus far we have been talking about natural prominence, which is carried by the relationship as such. However, the author can change the natural prominence if he so wishes. Each language has its own surface devices for doing this, and in such cases, the resultant prominence is referred to as *marked* prominence. Generally, the unit with marked prominence is considered to be of equal prominence with the naturally prominent unit. Thus, if a Reason unit is given prominence by the appropriate language devices, it will have equal prominence with the naturally prominent Result; if a Problem carries marked prominence, it will be equally prominent with the Resolution.

8.13.3 Natural prominence reversed by a dependency chain

The general statement can be made that a proposition or propositional configuration directly related to a Head can never be of lesser rank than a proposition or propositional configuration which is less directly related to the Head. That relationship marks it as of higher prominence than the other half of a binary relation, even if that half normally carries natural prominence.

An interesting example of this is found in 1 Tim. 2:1–7. In that paragraph, which consists of a number of clusters (seven are identified in the display), 2:4 is labeled as Grounds for 2:3, which, in turn is the Grounds for the Head. Verse 2:7 is the Result of 2:4. Normally, the Result is of higher rank than the Reason to which it is related, but here the Reason cluster in 2:4 is more closely related to the Head, and so the normal prominence is overruled by the closeness of relationship to the Head. Figure 8.31, using boxes for the propositional clusters, gives a pictorial representation of the above situation. The second pattern of boxes in the diagram would imply that 2:7 was directly supporting the Head, like 2:3, but this is not the case, so the second pattern is rejected as misleading.

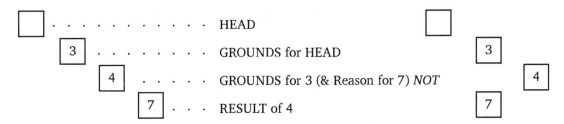

Figure 8.31. Reversal of natural prominence.

8.13.4 Conjoined units of unequal prominence

Communication units which are related to one another by Conjoining are normally of equal rank or prominence. Occasionally, however, a Conjoined unit is marked for lesser prominence. The analyst, therefore, needs to be aware that Conjoining does not invariably imply equal prominence. An example of this is found in a paragraph 4–7 of Philemon. In this paragraph there are three propositional clusters, the main propositions of which are each introduced by an Orienter. These are "I thank God..." (4), "I pray that..." (4), and "I rejoiced and was comforted that..." (7). However, the three clusters are not all equally prominent. By leaving the Orienter implicit in the second cluster, the author has signaled a lesser prominence for this propositional cluster. The relation is still one of Conjoining, but only two of the three conjoined units share the same degree of prominence.

CHART OF RELATIONS INVOLVING COMMUNICATION UNITS[1]

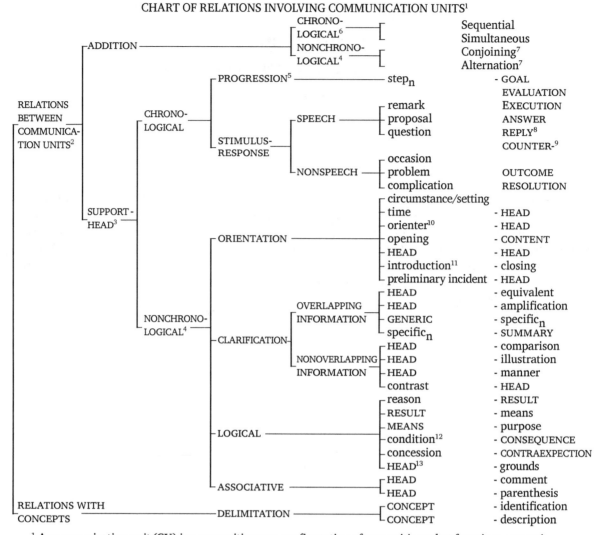

[1] A communication unit (CU) is a proposition or a configuration of propositions that functions as a unit.

[2] As a larger configuration is analyzed into its constituent CU's, each constituent will be found to be in some relation with at least one other constituent in that configuration, and each will have with respect to the other a role corresponding with that relationship.

[3] For a given pair of labels, the role of the CU having greater natural prominence is indicated in upper-case letters, and the role of the CU having lesser prominence is shown in lower case. The role labels for each pair are shown in the order in which the units more frequently occur in New Testament Greek texts.

[4] Nonchronological should not be taken to mean that there is no relative temporal relationship between the pair of CU's; rather, that the focus is not on the temporal notion.

[5] Often a sequence of events, usually performed by the same participant, lacks the feature of stimulus-response, yet involves a movement toward a more prominent event or goal. In such cases, this set of labels is needed.

[6] In a CU display, these labels will be used in conjunction with the label HEAD, e.g., sequential $HEAD_1$—sequential $HEAD_2$, or simultaneous $HEAD_1$—simultaneous $HEAD_2$.

[7] These labels will not normally be used in a CU display. Conjoining will be marked with subscript numbers following the head or support role label that the conjoined units have with respect to other units, e.g., $HEAD_1$—$HEAD_2$—etc. or $reason_1$—$reason_2$—etc. If alternation is involved, the units would be labeled as follows: alternate $HEAD_1$—alternate $HEAD_2$—etc. or alternate $reason_1$—alternate $reason_2$—etc.

[8] REPLY is a verbal response to any speech stimulus other than the response which naturally corresponds with that stimulus.

[9] For each speech stimulus, there is a corresponding counter-role response in which a different speaker, in response to a remark, proposal, question, etc., makes an alternative or substitute remark, proposal, question, etc.

This alternative or substitute is labeled COUNTERREMARK, COUNTERPROPOSAL, COUNTERQUESTION, etc. Within the bracketed sets, any one stimulus may be paired with any of the responses.

[10] Types of orienters are speech, perceptual, emotional, cognitive, volitional, evaluative, and prominence.

[11] Introduction includes topic orienter, preview (topic and part of the theme are stated), prologue (used in narrative genre). These more specific labels may be used at the discretion of the analyst.

[12] The condition element of this relation may be subdivided into three types: contrary to fact, potential fact:general, and potential fact:particular.

[13] The HEAD in this relation may be either an IMPLICATION/CONCLUSION (statement), an EXHORTATION (command), or a QUESTION. In relation to EXHORTATION, grounds will include motivation. Some analysts may prefer this more specific label.

9

THE PARAGRAPH AND LARGER UNITS IN NONNARRATIVE GENRES

The paragraph is the semantic unit which follows the propositional cluster in the semantic hierarchy; that is to say, typically, the main constituents of a paragraph are propositional clusters. "Typically" is used, however, because the hierarchical organization is not a rigid one, so propositions also may be major constituents of a paragraph. Like all semantic units, the paragraph is characterized by the three analytical and the three holistic features (see section 2.3). Furthermore, it is the information communicated by the paragraph that is the first to be classified in terms of the discourse genres. One way, then, of describing a paragraph would be: a paragraph is a combination of propositional clusters or propositions, which exhibits referential, situational, and structural coherence and prominence, and which either narrates a given topic, expounds it, exhorts it, gives directions concerning it, describes it, or relates conversations pertaining to it.

9.1 Coherence in the paragraph

As was stated in section 2.3.1, *referential and situational coherence* is based on:

1. Sameness of content, i.e., the recurrence of referential and situational meaning within the semantic unit;
2. Concepts from the same semantic and/or experiential domains.

   Since, in the identification of paragraphs in discourse, coherence plays an important part, types of evidence for coherence which can be expected in any language are listed below:

1. The same time, location, or topic being relevant to a sequence of propositions.
2. Repetition of a main animate participant (in any role) or repeated reference to a topic. Variations in repeating the reference to a concept or larger semantic unit can take the following forms:
   a. The concept may be repeated in the exact form and refer to the same referent. For example, "Joe...Joe."
   b. The concept may be repeated by use of different lexical items to refer to the same referent. For example, "The university's Student Council...the Council"; or (using a derived form) "Bill chose not to go...his choice."·
   c. Substitution forms (pronouns, pro-verbs). The substitution form is always different, but the referent is the same as its antecedent.
3. Synonymy. In synonymy the form is always different but the referent is the same. By definition, the referent in context is always the same for words that are considered synonymous.
4. Semantic domains. The forms are different and the referents are also different (even belonging to different semantic classes), but all are related by belonging to the same semantic domain; e. g. the Sea of Galilee, casting a net, lake, fishermen, boat (Mark 1:16–20).
5. Generic-specifics. The forms are different and the referents are also different, but all the specifics are included semantically in the generic class and are thus related; e.g., the fruit of the Spirit (generic); love, joy, peace, patience, etc. (specifics) (Gal. 5:22).
6. Experiential sets. The forms and referents are different. They do not necessarily share any components of meaning, but they belong to a single set by virtue of occurring together in a specific experience in the referential realm of the discourse; e. g. made an opening, roof, digging through, lowered, mat, paralyzed man (Mark 2:4).
7. Continuity of connotation and register.

8. Reciprocals. The forms are different, but the referents have considerable overlap since each recipro-cal pair refers to the same event from a different perspective; e. g. "we have heard...of the love you have"; "Epaphras...told us of your love" (Col. 1:3, 8).
9. Person, time/tense, mood. When these are repeated, they provide evidence for coherence.
10. The same relations (case or communication relations) repeated in a series.
11. Rhetorical structures such as parallelism, chiasmus, and sandwich structures, all of which involve patterned repetition of information (i.e., a combination of referential and structural coherence).

Structural coherence, as stated in section 2.3.1, is based on:

1. The collocational compatibility of the constituents in the referential realm of the communication; and
2. The appropriateness of the relations (explicit or implicit) which tie the constituents of a semantic unit together.

Structural coherence within a paragraph is expressed by means of what may be called a *logic line*. A logic line is formed when a head proposition or propositional cluster is directly or indirectly supported by other propositions or propositional clusters. However, two propositions or propositional clusters which are related to one another by such relations as Reason-Result, Contrast, etc., possess coherence by consisting of propositions which are appropriate to fill the roles assigned to them by the relational structure. This proper selection of units for their roles is a characteristic of structural coherence. The relations will often be signaled by conjunctions and other types of connectors, forming a grammatical *dependency chain* in the surface structure, giving expression to the logic line.

Surface-structure forms, therefore, such as conjunctions, prepositions, case markers, pronouns, deictics, same or different subject markers, etc., all serve to signal the structural coherence of a paragraph or larger unit.

9.2 Paragraph boundaries and Koiné Greek surface structure

Because of the importance of the paragraph in discourse, especially nonnarrative discourse, in addition to the above descriptions of referential, situational, and structural coherence, a further section is added here on surface structure features in Koiné Greek which help to identify paragraphs, especially by indi-cating their boundaries. Surface-structure signals which under certain circumstances are known to have this function are given below:

1. Generic previews (1 Cor. 7:1)
2. Rhetorical questions (Rom. 6:1, 15)
3. Forefronted topics (1 Cor. 2:6; 1 Tim. 5:3; 6:1) or participants (Col. 1:21; 2:13)
4. Sandwich structures (Col. 1:3, 8; 1:3, 12; 1:3–5; and 2:5)
5. Parallelism (Col. 2:20 and 3:1)
6. Vocatives (Jude 3, 17)
7. Orienters—speech (1 Cor. 1:4, 10) and nonspeech (1 Thess. 5:13)
8. Conjunctions which can occur paragraph initial, such as *oun* 'therefore', *de* 'but/and', *kai* 'and', *gar* 'for', and *dio* 'therefore'
9. Tail-head transitions, i.e., information at the end of one paragraph repeated near the beginning of the next paragraph (1 Cor. 2:5, 6 (*sophia* 'wisdom'); Col. 1:5–6 (*euaggelion* 'gospel'))
10. Genitive absolutes 1 Thess.3:6)
11. Topic-announcing devices—*peri de...* 'now concerning...' (1 Cor. 7:1; 8:1; 12:1; 1 Thess. 4:9; 5:1)

Some further comment is needed on *tail-head transitions*. The examples quoted are of a concept found near the end of one unit and then repeated near the beginning of the following unit. This type of *lexical tail-head link* signals what is known as a "seam" between the two units. In other words, while the lineal connection between the two concepts is clear, there is equally evidently a clear break between the two units. The concept does not need to be repeated in its full surface form, as in the examples cited above; it may be repeated using a relative pronoun, as in Col. 1:13 and 15.

There is, however, another type of tail-head connection between paragraphs, a *relational tail-head transition*, which is likely to cause the analyst more difficulty. When a conjunction is used to relate the last proposition or propositional cluster of one paragraph to the first proposition or propositional cluster of the following paragraph, we have a relational tail-head transition. The problem which this presents to the analyst is a clash between the transitional relation between the two paragraphs and the relation between the thematic content of the two paragraphs. The two sometimes clash since the latter is based on the relation that holds between the main proposition(s) of each paragraph; whereas the relational tail-head transition is usually based on the relation between a closing support proposition of one paragraph and the initial proposition of the next, which may or may not be the main proposition. This is an instance where the lineal character of language introduces a relation which is skewed relative to the hierarchical relations between the units. Normally a head proposition relates to a head proposition. When a closing support proposition is related to a head proposition, this serves as a transition, but does not indicate the relation between the two paragraphs.

Two possible examples of this type of tail-head transition are 2 Tim. 1:6 and Col. 1:9. 2 Tim. 1:6 begins with *di' hēn aitian* 'for which reason' and it would be expected, if it were linking the two paragraphs consisting of 1:3–5 and 1:6–7 together, that these paragraphs would be in the relation of Reason-Result or Grounds-Conclusion. But 1:3–5 is analyzed as the Introduction to the Body of 2 Timothy, which begins with 1:6. Hence, "for which reason" is considered to be linking 1:5 and 6, and perhaps more particularly the end of 1:5 to 1:6. Timothy's faith, which is referred to at the end of 1:5, is the Grounds for Paul urging Timothy to fan his spiritual gift into flame.

Col. 1:9 is somewhat similar. The opening *dia touto* 'for this reason' is not the relation between paragraphs 1:3–8 and 1:9–12, which in fact are related by Conjoining. Rather, *dia touto* relates back to the report that Epaphras had brought to Paul (mentioned in 1:8).

Figure 9.1 presents some of the evidence that was used to determine the boundaries of a number of paragraphs in Colossians. The evidence is divided into two groups—that drawn from coherence features, and that contributed by Koiné Greek boundary-marking devices. What is of particular interest is that Section 1 (1:3–29) is an expository unit, whereas Section 2 (2:6–3:17) is a hortatory unit, and this difference of genre shows up in various ways on the chart, especially in the boundary-marking devices.

	SC	tail-head	sandwich	οὖν	special closure patterns
S E C T I O N 1	1		✓		
	2	✓			✓
	3	✓	✓		
	4	✓			
	5	✓	✓		
S E C T I O N 2	1		✓	✓	✓
	2				
	3			✓	✓
	4				
	5		✓	✓	
	6			✓	
	7				✓
	8				
	9				✓

Figure 9.1. Criteria used in identifying boundaries
of section constituents in Colossians.

In the chart, SC = Section Constituent. The constituents of Section 1 are SC1 1:3–8; SC2 1:9–12; SC3 1:13–20; SC4 1:21–23; SC5 1:24–29. The constituents of Section 2 are SC1 2:6–7; SC2 2:8–15; SC3 2:16–19; SC4 2:20–23; SC5 3:1–4; SC6 3:5–11; SC7 3:12–15; SC8 3:16; SC9 3:17; The check (√) symbol indicates that the criterion was used in establishing one or the other boundary of that particular constituent.

9.3 The classification of the information communicated by paragraphs

As mentioned above, the paragraph is the smallest propositional configuration whose information can be classed in terms of the various discourse genres. This gives a broad classification into the four major types of narration, exhortation, exposition, and procedure, with the two minor types of description and dialogue. Our studies have shown that, in general, a group of paragraphs—e.g., a section, episode, scene—shares the same discourse genre, so that genre change will often mark a high-level boundary.

The detailed illocutionary subclassification of the proposition (section 2.3.2) is equally applicable to the paragraph. Paragraphs may be subclassed as thanksgiving, prayer (both common in the Epistles), explanation, advertisement, consolation, correction, an order, warning, request, admonition, etc. Unless the discourse being analyzed is very long, e.g., a novel, history, biography, etc., the variety of subclassifications is likely to be restricted by the subject matter of the discourse. But in general, the subclassification of paragraphs is an open set, reflecting the great variety of topics that discourses are about.

9.4 The role of paragraphs

Since a paragraph is a propositional configuration with a function in a higher-level unit, typically the section, its role may be any of the communication roles described in the preceding chapter. It could be Grounds, Equivalent, Specific, Introduction, etc., in nonnarrative material; Setting, Occasion, Problem, etc., in narrative.

Since propositions may relate to concepts, it could be expected that paragraphs might also relate to propositions. This, in fact, is what is occasionally found in text material. A paragraph may relate to part of another paragraph rather than to the whole paragraph; that is, a paragraph may be related to a concept or a proposition in another paragraph. And that concept or proposition may not be the head or part of the head of that paragraph. In such cases, the paragraph fills either a delimiting or explanatory function which the author felt important to include.

An example of this is found in 1 Tim. 1:8–11. These verses constitute a paragraph on the topic of the law, which is a concept referred to negatively in a support proposition of 1:3–7, the preceding paragraph (see 1:7). The paragraph gives a positive description of the law in order to correct any misunderstanding that might otherwise arise from the negative remark made in 1:7. The descriptive function of the paragraph, while not related to the head of the preceding paragraph, is nevertheless important in the development of the total theme and purpose of the section of which it is a part.

9.5 Prominence and thematic content in the paragraph

9.5.1 Natural prominence and the theme

Like each of the semantic units, the paragraph has a structural center to which the main constituents of the paragraph are directly related. In the case of the paragraph, this center constitutes the main part of the *theme*. It consists of the main proposition(s) to which all the other propositions, via the main propositional clusters, are related. If the structural center is introduced by an Orienter, this Orienter can also form part of the theme. For example, if "he promised that he would come (because)…" were the center of a paragraph, then the theme would include the Orienter "he promised" as well as the Content, "he would come"; the Content without the Orienter would not make any sense as the theme.

The indication of the main proposition(s) is one aspect of the prominence system of a paragraph. The normal pattern by which prominence is indicated is referred to as *natural prominence*. This means that the manner in which the prominence is indicated follows the course of greatest economy in communication, by using the central constituent as the proposition in focus, usually signaled by the natural means of grammatical subordination.

9.5.2 Marked prominence

In addition to the main proposition(s) (the structural center) of the paragraph, indicated by the patterns of natural prominence, there may also be *marked prominence*—that is to say, highlighting (focus) prominence—on some proposition. If the marked proposition(s) is directly related to the main proposition(s), then, because of its marked prominence, it becomes part of the theme for that paragraph. That is to say, the theme of a paragraph consists of the naturally prominent main proposition(s), together with any highlighted proposition that is directly related to the main one.

Every language has its own prominence devices, which the translator needs to master. Some of the devices used in New Testament Greek to give marked prominence to propositions are briefly discussed below.

A *nominalized (and/or forefronted) relation* may be used to show marked prominence. In 1 Tim. 1:5 *telos* 'end' represents Purpose, and its forefronted position gives prominence to the Purpose. In 1 Thess. 2:13 *dia touto* 'on account of this' refers forward to the *hoti* 'because' following the verb of thanks, and it gives prominence to the Reason for the thanks. Both of these are examples of *cataphora* (reference to something ahead in the text), which is another means of showing special prominence. *Rhetorical questions* are used to make emphatic statements (though they can also be used to "tone down" the pointedness of a command or negative evaluation). *Proportion*, that is to say, extent of development, can also give prominence, but it is a difficult factor to evaluate. Recent research in narration indicates that *direct speech in summary form* may be a prominence device in that genre.

There are two rather special devices used in Greek, which can also show prominence. These are sandwich and chiastic structures.

Sandwich structures, also known as *inclusio*, occur when the beginning and end of a unit share enough information and/or surface structure form to make it very probable that such a structure is more than a coincidence. Such structures, along with other factors, serve to indicate the boundaries of units, whether of a paragraph or a larger combination of units. When a sandwich structure is based primarily on information content or could be considered such, apart from formal similarities, it functions not only to indicate the beginning and end of the unit but also to indicate what is in focus. For example, 1 Tim. 1:3–8 deals with the charge and its purpose; 1 Tim. 1:18–20 refers again to the charge. This sandwich structure shows that the charge is prominent in this combination of paragraphs. A further example is found in Col. 1:24–29. Verses 1:24 and 25, on the one hand, and 1:28 and 29, on the other, form a sandwich structure, since both have to do with Paul's ministry. This sandwich structure shows that the focus is on Paul's ministry, and not on the mystery which is described in 1:26 and 27.

Chiastic structures may be designed for stylistic purposes, but those which have been analyzed up to the present serve the same functions as the sandwich structure. Since the chiastic structure is more fully explained elsewhere (see Beekman and Callow 1974:226–227), suffice it to say here that, in such structures, not only are the ends semantically related but so also are the middle parts. Thus, the structure is frequently represented as ABBA, with other more intricate variations of the same basic form being found. When there is an even number of parts, the outer parts tend to be prominent (e.g., ABCCBA); if the number of parts is uneven, the center tends to be the place of prominence (ABCBA).

The prominence function of chiastic structure was described over one hundred years ago. In his book, *Symmetrical Structure of Scripture* (1854:45, 57–58), John Forbes gives two examples of chiasmus in the New Testament, drawing on the writings of Bishop Jebb. One is from Rom. 2:12–15 (figure 9.2) and the other is from Heb. 7:27–28 (figure 9.3). Concerning the chiastic structure of Rom. 2:12–15, he comments (1854:45):

> Here, according to the principles of the Epanados [= chiasmus], the case of the Gentiles is put first and last (A and A'), as furnishing the strongest apparent objection to the equity of the doctrine laid down by the Apostle, that 'all are under sin, and brought in as guilty before God'; while the statement with regard to the Jews' guilt (B), and its proof (B'), are placed in the middle and subordinate place.

His comment (1854:58) on the Heb. 7:27–28 passage is:

> The non-necessity of offering for his own sins, is *first* asserted, and *last* proved, in order to give prominence to the *grand* distinctions between him and the legal high priests.

A   All who sin apart from the law will also perish apart from the law,

  B   and all who sin under the law will be judged by the law.

  B'   Those who hear and obey the law are righteous.

A'   Although the Gentiles do not have the law, they obey it.

Figure 9.2. Chiastic structure of Rom. 2:12–15.

A   Unlike the other high priests, he does not need to offer sacrifices day after day, first for his
     own sins,

    B   and then for the sins of the people;

    B'   for he sacrificed for their sins once for all when he offered himself.

A'   For the law appoints as high priests men who are weak, but the oath, which came after the
     law, appointed the Son, who has been made perfect for evermore.

Figure 9.3. Chiastic structure of Heb. 7:27–28.

9.5.3 The topic

The theme of a paragraph is always (at least) a proposition, and so, like all propositions, it consists of a topic and the comment. This topic, then, is the main (thematic) topic of the paragraph, and consequently it will be referred to repeatedly in the paragraph, using some of the coherence devices listed in section 9.1. In fact, one particular and important aspect of redundancy of information in the paragraph is repeated reference to the paragraph topic. Looked at from a different perspective, that topic which is referred to at various points in the paragraph is very likely to be the paragraph topic.

In the extensive discussion of topic in section 6.3.3, a distinction was drawn between natural and marked topics. It follows from that discussion that the topic of a paragraph (or larger unit) may also be natural or marked. In the Greek of the New Testament, various surface-structure devices are used to mark topics, some of which have already been referred to (in general) in section 6.3.3, e.g., use of the passive, and nominalization of Event and Attribute concepts. In addition, in Greek there is the common device of forefronting, i.e., placing the nominal phrase that represents the topic before the verb in the clause. Since the natural topic and topics marked by the use of the passive are in the nominative case in Greek, forefronted topics are generally in the accusative, genitive, or dative case (though a topic in the genitive case seems rather less likely). Examples of forefronted paragraph topics in the accusative case are found in 1 Cor. 2:6 (*sophian* 'wisdom'); 4:1 (*hēmas* 'us'); Col. 3:1–2 (*ta anō* 'the things above'); 1 Tim. 5:3 (*chēras* 'widows'). An example of a forefronted topic in the dative case (in this case only part of the paragraph topic) is found in 1 Tim. 5:1, *presbuterō* 'an elder'.

The function of the passive construction is to topicalize concepts functioning in the roles of Affectant, Beneficiary, or Instrument. In units where a concept is the Affectant of a commanded Event, a device used in Greek to topicalize it is the third person imperative form (which allows the retention of the imperative mood) with a forefronted subject that represents the Affectant concept. Consider, for example, Col. 3:16. It reads, *ho logos tou Christou enoikeitō en humin plousiōs* 'Continue getting to know very well the message (topic) about Christ'. The concept with the role of Affectant is "the message about Christ" and this is represented by the subject phrase *ho logos tou Christou* 'the word of Christ' in the surface structure.

When a Topic Orienter (one of the orientation roles) is used to identify and announce the topic, that topic is considered marked. Examples of this are found in 1 Cor. 12:1 and 16:1, where the forefronted *peri de...* 'now concerning...' phrase introduces the topics of spiritual gifts and the collection for the saints, respectively.

It was stated earlier that the topic would be repeatedly and redundantly referred to throughout a paragraph or larger unit. One of the examples of a marked topic that was given earlier was *sophia* 'wisdom' in 1 Cor. 2:6. The paragraph of which this is the topic runs from 2:6 to 2:8, and in every clause, except the last two, the concept of *sophia* 'wisdom' is explicitly referred to, either by the noun itself, or by the concordant article *tēn* or the concordant relative pronoun *hēn*. The next to last clause in 2:8 is *ei gar egnōsan* 'for if they had known', and the implicit object is clearly "wisdom," from the preceding clause. Only the final clause has no reference, overt or covert, to wisdom. This sequence of references to *sophian* shows that the forefronted *sophian* in the first clause of 2:6 is not simply the topic for that clause, but for the whole paragraph.

9.5.4　Theme and its surface structure representation

The following discussion is based on the assumption that the Greek speaker reacted to clues in the surface structure which told him what the theme was for any given paragraph. Our task is to identify those clues. The following suggestions are put forward:

1. If the main clause represents an Orienter, then the theme consists primarily of the Content of the Orienter. The Content may be represented by either (a) an accusative + infinitive clause following the Orienter, or (b) a *hina* or *hoti* 'that' clause following the Orienter, provided that none of these clauses has a verb which represents a second Orienter, in which case the theme consists of the (main) Content of the second Orienter.
2. If there is no Orienter, then the theme is signaled by the main clause in the paragraph. When there is a series of coordinated main clauses forming a single paragraph, all of which are semantically related by Conjoining and thus are of equal prominence, then the theme is either abstracted from the series, or a theme consisting of Conjoined propositions is required.

Undoubtedly, this is too simple a statement. The following discussion of paragraph themes in 1 Timothy and Colossians will help to clarify the definitions and point out problem spots.

9.5.4.1　*Themes that derive from central constituents with an explicit Orienter*

a. Orienter with accusative and infinitive clause

1 Tim. 2:1–7

Orienter:	*Parakalō oun prōton pantōn* 'I urge, then, first of all' (2:1)
Content:	*poieisthai, deēseis, proseuchas, enteuxeis, eucharistias, huper pantōn anthrōpōn* 'that requests, prayers, intercessions, and thanksgiving be made for everyone' (2:1)

There is another independent clause in this paragraph in 2:3: *Touto kalon kai apodekton enōpion tou sōtēros hēmōn theou* 'this (is) good and acceptable before God our Savior'. It is not the theme, however, since it is not directly related to the Orienter but to the Content or its development, depending on what *touto* 'this' refers to. It is probably a general rule that a medial deictic of this sort cannot be part of the theme: it would have to be paragraph initial or final.

1 Tim. 2:8–15

Orienter:	*Boulomai oun* 'I want, then' (2:8)
Content:	*proseuchesthai tous andras (en panti topō), epairontas hosious cheiras* 'men (everywhere) to lift up holy hands in prayer' (2:8)
Orienter:	*Hōsautōs [kai]* 'Similarly (also)' (2:9)
Content:	*gunaikas en katastolē kosmiō...kosmein heautas* 'I want women to dress modestly' (2:9)

Here is a paragraph with two Orienters and Contents, joined by *hōsautōs [kai]* 'similarly' (also) (the *kai* is textually indeterminate—hence the brackets). In this paragraph, *hōsautōs* 'similarly' is an anaphoric device to repeat the initial Orienter *boulomai* 'I want'. This is confirmed by the accusative and infinitive construction following *hōsautōs*. In the semantic-structure analysis of 1 Timothy (Blight 1977), the theme for 2:8–15 combines these two Contents into a Conjoined theme statement "good men are to pray and women are to wear modest clothing."

1 Tim. 3:1–7

Orienter:	*dei oun* 'It is necessary, then' (3:2)
Content:	*ton episkopon anepilēmpton einai* 'that an overseer be above reproach' (3:2)

Dei 'it is necessary' is one form of impersonal Orienter. *Ton episkopon* 'the overseer' is not analyzed as forefronted, since subject-complement-verb is Paul's normal order for *einai* 'to be' clauses. The interesting question here is: What is the function of 3:1, if 3:2 gives the Orienter plus theme? Verse 3:1 is either a prominence Orienter, drawing attention to the important topic of overseer, or a Preview of the topic, or both.

1 Tim. 3:8–13

> Orienter: *hōsautōs* 'similarly' (3:8)
> Content: *diakonous...* 'deacons (must be)...' (3:8)

Hōsautōs 'similarly' refers back to the Orienter *dei* 'it is necessary' in 3:2; and *einai* 'to be' is ellipsed. However, there is a minor problem in that the qualifications that are given, starting with *semnous* 'worthy of respect', are specific, giving no generic theme. The simplest solution is to say that not only is *einai* ellipsed, but so also is *anepilēmpton* 'above reproach', so that *hōsautōs* replaces the full form **dei diakonous anepilēmpton einai...* 'it is necessary that deacons be above reproach...'

b. Orienter plus *hoti* 'that'

1 Tim. 4:1–5

> Orienter: *To de pneuma rētōs legei* 'The Spirit clearly says' (4:1)
> Content: *hoti en husterois kairois apostēsontai tines tēs pisteōs* 'that in later times some will abandon the faith' (4:1)

In this case, the Orienter uses a verb of speaking and so is followed by *hoti* 'that' and a clause with a finite indicative verb. The theme is the Content.

c. Orienter plus *hina* 'that'

1 Cor. 14:13–19

> Orienter: *ho lalōn glōssē proseuchesthō...* 'let the one who speaks in a tongue pray...' (14:13)
> Content: *hina diermēneuē* 'that he may interpret' (14:13)

Here, the Orienter uses a prayer verb (one of the many urgent expressions of will—to want, wish, urge, desire, implore, etc.—which require a subjunctive clause linked by *hina* to express their Content (see Werner 1981). The main part of the theme is the Content.

9.5.4.2. *Themes that derive from central constituents involving third person commands*

The assumption is made that third person commands are a surface-structure representation of a second person command. However, the choice of a third person command rather than a second person one seems rather to be a topicalizing device.

The sequence of paragraphs in 1 Tim. 5 (5:3; 5:4–8; 5:9–10; 5:11–15; 5:16) all give instructions of one sort and another concerning widows. That is to say, the common topic of these five paragraphs is "widows." Note the form of the thematic information in the first, third, and fifth paragraphs:

5:3 *chēras tima tas ontōs chēras* 'honor widows who are genuinely widows' (5:3)—second person command, with *chēras* 'widows' forefronted, signaling the topic for this sequence of paragraphs.
5:9–10 *chēra katalegesthō...* 'let a widow be enrolled...' (5:9) (*chēra* 'widow ' is forefronted and is the subject of a third person command)
5:11–15 *neōteras de chēras paraitou* 'reject younger widows' (5:11) (*chēras* 'widows' is forefronted in a second person command)

It seems reasonable to assume that the form used in 5:9, with a third person command and forefronted subject, *chēra* 'widow', is semantically equivalent to the form used in the other two, where *chēras* 'widows' is the forefronted object of a second person command, and that in each case the surface structure is signaling that *chēra(s)* 'widow(s)' is the topic.

9.6 Simple, complex, and compound paragraphs

Since the paragraph is a propositional configuration in the same way that the propositional cluster is, it would be a reasonable expectation that the structural patterns discussed for the propositional cluster (section 7.2) would be broadly paralleled in the paragraph; this proves to be the case.

A *simple paragraph* is one in which each main constituent (proposition or propositional cluster is directly related to the head constituent.

A *complex paragraph* is rather more difficult to describe. Consider the case in which, using the clues provided by the semantic and surface structures, two contiguous paragraphs are identified. When, however, the content and role of the second of the two paragraphs are studied and analyzed, it is found that it is not related to the head of the first paragraph but to one of the constituents supporting that head. To make this situation clearer, consider figure 9.4, in which solid lines enclose identified paragraphs, broken lines enclose identified propositional clusters, and arrows show support roles. In this type of situation, the second paragraph is not a major constituent of the first, since it is not related to the head cluster. At the same time, it is not a propositional cluster, as is shown by various evidence[s]. In fact, the analysis is that it is supporting a constituent (or part of a constituent) in the first paragraph. Then, the combination of these two paragraphs would be described as a complex paragraph.

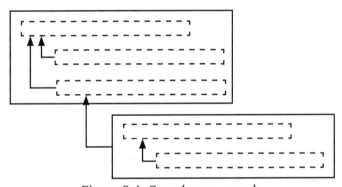

Figure 9.4. Complex paragraph.

A possible example of this complex type of structure has been encountered in 1 Tim. 1:8–11. This unit is a paragraph dealing with the topic of the law, and it is analyzed as supporting part or all of the last constituent of the preceding paragraph (1:3–7).

In defining simple and complex forms of the propositional cluster, it was stated that a propositional cluster had to consist of at least two propositions, otherwise it would not be a configuration at all. A similar minimum condition is proposed for a paragraph, i.e., it must consist of at least two constituents, one of which is a propositional cluster and the other of which may be either a proposition or propositional cluster.

There are several possible forms which a minimum paragraph could take. These are diagrammed in figure 9.5, using lines to represent propositions, boxes to represent propositional clusters, and a dotted line to represent an implicit proposition.

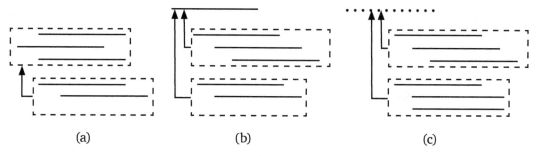

Figure 9.5. Forms of minimum paragraphs.

In form (a) both the head and the support are propositional clusters. In (b) the head is a single proposition, but it is supported by two propositional clusters. In (c) two propositional clusters are related by Conjoining, so an abstracted head is proposed, to which the two propositional clusters are related. In other words, (b) and (c) differ in that (b) has an explicit head and (c) has an implicit head.

Example (a), however, raises some theoretical questions, which are not possible to answer entirely satisfactorily at this stage in the development of the theory. The question can be asked, concerning the head propositional cluster, as to why the two supporting propositions, one preceding and one following, are not treated as major constituents, separate from the main proposition. Put in diagram form, why is example (a) not diagrammed as (a') in figure 9.6? With this analysis, there would be three main constituents, two being propositions and the third a cluster. Further, if it were so analyzed, would it still be a paragraph?

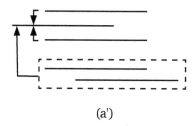

(a')

Figure 9.6. Alternate of (a) (figure 9.5).

In answer to these questions, the following can be said:

1. If the diagram (a') were a correct display of the analysis of the unit consisting of five propositions, then it could be either a minimal paragraph or a complex propositional cluster. Which it is will be determined on other grounds (see section 7.1).
2. It seems to be intuitively the case that propositions with certain roles are more closely tied to the head proposition than units with other roles.

    Roles in this category appear to include Circumstance, Orienter, Manner, Identification, and Description; and may possibly include Equivalence, Amplification, and Specific. The implication of this approach would be that a propositional cluster with the role of Reason would support not just the single main proposition, but its Circumstance, Orienter, etc. as well; or if the main proposition had an Equivalent, or a Specific proposition related to it, it would support the combination. It needs to be emphasized, however, that this possible distinction between the roles is largely intuitive at the moment, and that the above statements do no more than indicate which way the theory may go in seeking to account for these intuitions.

As was pointed out in the chapter on the propositional cluster (section 7.1), there is an overlap in structure between certain paragraphs and complex clusters. In such cases, where there is structural ambiguity, a final decision is made on the basis of the higher-level unit of which the problematical unit is a constituent. If it is a constituent of a paragraph, it is analyzed as a propositional cluster; if it is a constituent of a section, then it is regarded as a paragraph.

A *compound paragraph* is one in which there are two or more head propositional clusters related by the addition relation of Conjoining. This is found most commonly in hortatory genre, in which a series of commands are added to each other, without distinctions of prominence.

9.7 The theme of compound paragraphs

Compound paragraphs are essentially of two types. In one, the content of the Conjoined head propositions is such that they can be coalesced into one proposition. In the other, the head propositions are each fully represented (or sufficiently in detail to be considered fully represented) in the statement of the theme, rather than being "fused" into a single thematic proposition.

9.7.1 A theme with a single main proposition abstracted from a compound paragraph

An expository paragraph may have two or more main propositions which are briefly developed. An example of this occurs in Phlm. 4–7, where the main propositions of verses 4–6 are "I thank God because you believe in the Lord Jesus and love all the saints" and the main propositions of verse 7 are "I rejoice and am encouraged because you love the saints." These main propositions are so closely related with the repetition of the Reason proposition "you love (all) the saints" and with the Orienters, which give related aspects of Paul's attitude, that verses 4–7 may be considered a compound paragraph with an abstracted theme "I was moved because you love all the saints." For two or more propositional clusters to be considered as constituting a compound paragraph with a single-proposition theme, their main propositions must (1) be closely related in content, (2) be in a Conjoining relation to one another, (3) be of equal rank semantically, and (4) serve the same function with respect to the unit of which the compound paragraph is a constituent.

Hortatory paragraphs are frequently compound. The author adds one command to another without any development or with only brief development. The unity of such a sequence of commands, however, derives from the fact that it is addressed to the same person(s) and deals with one semantic domain, such as ethical behavior or teaching ministry; and so a single theme can usually be abstracted. See, for example, 1 Tim. 4:12–15. In the semantic-structure analysis of 1 Timothy (Blight 1977), this paragraph has not less than twelve commands, and from these the theme is abstracted, "Show the believers by example how they should conduct themselves." Procedural paragraphs similarly are compound in structure and usually may be reduced to a single-proposition theme.

Descriptive paragraphs may serve to introduce a letter or to give a setting to a narrative, or an expanded description of a concept at any point in a discourse. In any case, an abstracted theme is likely to be based on a composite of significant participants or features of the setting (time, location, circumstance).

9.7.2 A theme with more than one main proposition taken from a compound paragraph

The compound paragraph discussed in the previous section resulted in a theme with a single main proposition, as did also the example from Philemon. The type of compound paragraph now under discussion results in a compound statement of theme. There are two or more distinct main propositions in a Conjoining relation serving as the theme. Even though the main propositions are related and have the same function, they cannot be reduced to a single main proposition without the loss of significant thematic information. The paragraph cited earlier from Philemon could have been considered a paragraph with a compound theme rather than one with a single abstracted theme. However, in that particular case, the information loss in the abstraction process was not considered to be significant in the development of the paragraph. This leads to the decision to abstract a theme with a single main proposition. The evidence needs to be weighed carefully when judging whether the theme of units consisting of closely related constituents is to be stated as a single main proposition by the process of abstraction or stated in compound form. The choice which is made is based on whether or not the main proposition of each constituent is independently relevant and essential to the progress of the unit.

Examples of this type of problem are found in Col. 3:1 and 3:2. Verse 3:1 has the command *ta anō zēteite* 'seek the things above', and 3:2 has the Conjoined command *ta anō phroneite* 'set your minds on things above'. Should the theme statement for paragraph 3:1–4 have a single main proposition abstracted from these two commands, or should the theme be compound? A similar problem is found in paragraph 3:5–12 of Colossians which has the Conjoined heads "put to death earthly deeds" (3:5) and "put off all (these earthly deeds)" (3:8). In both these cases, a theme with a single main proposition was abstracted.

9.8 Paragraph clusters

In the process of analyzing a discourse, the analyst will find the following type of situation. A section has been identified, and is analyzed as having four main constituents, that is to say, four spans of material, one of which is the head, and the other three directly support that head. Of these four constituents, the head and two of the supporting spans have the structural characteristics of a paragraph, which is what would be expected for the constituents of a section. But the fourth span of discourse is not a paragraph, but what appears to be three paragraphs conjoined to each other and of equal rank. In other words, these three paragraphs together, functioning as a unit of some sort, have a single role within the paragraph, parallel with the function of the individual paragraphs. If boxes are used for paragraphs, then the structural pattern of this section would be something like figure 9.7. How, then, should the span of three paragraphs be referred to? The proposed answer is, as a *paragraph cluster*. In general, then, for the paragraph and units higher in the semantic hierarchy, the term *cluster* refers to a group of two or more units, related by Conjoining and of equal rank, which have a single role (i.e., they function as a unit) parallel to individual units of the same level. It is because of the recursive nature of all propositional configurations that this "clustering" phenomenon is found at all levels in the semantic hierarchy.

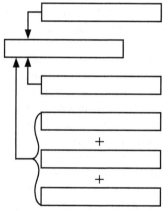

Figure 9.7. Paragraph cluster.

It should be noted that the basis for compounding and clustering is essentially the same, i.e., units linked by Conjoining and of equal rank. Compounding, however, refers to the presence of more than one head constituent in a unit; clustering refers to a group of support units which function within a unit as if they were only a single support unit.

9.9 The purpose of the paragraph

Depending on the way an author develops a section, the individual paragraphs may or may not have a purpose that can be stated in propositional form. If they do, then, since a paragraph may be classed as any of the discourse types, it may have any purpose that the author may have in mind when formulating the discourse. The purpose may be explicitly stated in the paragraph, or it may have to be deduced from the theme of the paragraph and its genre, since, apart from narrative genre, the very choice of a particular genre restricts the author's purpose. Narrative genre essentially tells a story, but a story may be told with a great variety of purposes in mind, so that the genre gives very little clue as to the author's purpose. But hortatory genre, for example, by its very nature, is urging, warning, advising, etc.; and so the author's purpose is restricted by that fact. Some of the purposes that a paragraph may have are listed below:

advise	confess	frighten	remind/review
agree	convince	forgive	restrain
amuse	criticize	impress	shame
annoy	defend	inform/teach	strengthen
answer	demand	oppose	support
appeal to	delegate x to y	pacify	surrender
arouse	embarrass	praise	test
accuse	encourage	prepare x for y	thank
boast	excite	prevent	threaten
betray	examine	promise	trap
comfort	expose	rebuke	warn
complain	flatter	reject	

9.10 Summary

The paragraph is a combination of two or more constituents, one of which is a propositional cluster. It exhibits referential, situational, and structural coherence, and it describes, narrates, expounds, exhorts, gives directions, questions, or relates conversations, in relation to a topic or theme. (See the chart of the analytical and holistic features of the paragraph, figure 9.8.)

ANALYTICAL FEATURES	UNITY: Two or more constituents, one of which is a proposi-tional cluster and the others of which are propositions and/or propositional clus-ters, combine to develop what is conceptualized as a single theme.	INTERNAL COHERENCE: Constituents which are compatible in the referential world, the communication situation, and the discourse structure are related in an appropriate manner using communication relations.	PROMINENCE: Natural relative prominence between the interrelated con-stituents isolates one or more head propositions or proposi-tional clusters from the other constituents that support it. Marked prominence may highlight one or more sup-porting constituents.
HOLISTIC FEATURES	CLASS: It may be a narrative, pro-cedure, exposition, exhorta-tion, description, or dialogue. (See discus-sion of proposition for subclassifications.)	EXTERNAL COHERENCE: As a compatible and appro-priately related constituent of a higher-level unit, it may serve either as the head or as a support unit, with any of the communication roles.	THEMATIC CONTENT: The central proposition or propositional cluster with or without an orien-ter, plus any highlighted proposition(s) constitute the thematic content which contributes to the purpose of the unit to inform, per-suade, encourage, amuse, ridicule, greet, praise, etc.

Figure 9.8. The meaning features of the paragraph.

This suggests that, based on the discourse genre of a paragraph, there are the following general paragraph types.

Descriptive paragraphs (e.g., settings, travelogues)
Narrative paragraphs (e.g., stories)
Expository paragraphs (e.g., explanations, definitions, interpretations)
Hortatory paragraphs (e.g., arguments, persuasion, direct imperatives)
Procedural paragraphs (e.g., how-to articles)
Interrogative paragraphs (e.g., cross-examinations of witnesses by a lawyer)
Dialogue paragraphs (e.g., committee discussions)

More specific genre and subgenre classifications of paragraph types are not only possible but desirable for greater precision.

A paragraph has a prominent structural center and may have marked focus in addition. This center consists of the main proposition(s) together with an Orienter that is thematic. Marked focus is indicated by the prominence signals of the language and may be different from the center. The structural center of a paragraph, together with any main constituent that is marked as prominent, constitutes the theme for that paragraph.

(The term "paragraph," throughout this theory, has been used of a semantic unit with well-defined characteristics. The term, however, is very widely used of printed or graphic paragraphs, and, depending on factors such as the genre being printed, and the paragraphing policy of the writer, graphic paragraphs can vary in length from one-word replies, such as "Yeah" or "Sure" or "Fine," through single clauses or sentences, to much longer stretches. What is being discussed in this theory is the identification of a particular semantic unit in a discourse, not a policy for graphic paragraphs.)

9.11 Units larger than the paragraph in nonnarrative genres

Many discourses will consist of only one or two paragraphs. This is true especially in oral communication. In written communication, however, most discourses involve a large number of paragraphs. According to the "packaging" principle (see section 1.5.2), these paragraphs are grouped together, just as propositional clusters are grouped together into paragraphs. And each semantic unit so formed will exhibit all of the six meaning features described for the paragraph (figure 9.8). In other words, the summary presentation of the meaning features of the paragraph could be very easily modified to apply to units higher in the hierarchy; there would be no essential difference. However, it should be borne in mind that the higher a unit is in the semantic hierarchy, the more possibility there is for its constituents to be "mixed." For example, a section typically consists of paragraphs, but it may also have constituents which are propositional clusters, or even a single proposition.

The following hierarchy is suggested for nonnarrative materials (the next chapter will suggest a hierarchy for narrative):

paragraph ====➔ section ====➔ division ====➔ part

(The arrow (====➔) points "up" the hierarchy.) If a discourse is analyzed and is found to be long enough or complex enough to require units higher than a part, then the analyst is at liberty to choose appropriate labels, according to the type of discourse, for such higher-level units.

In the semantic-structure analysis of 1 Timothy (Blight 1977), the body of the epistle (which includes all of the Epistle except the opening two verses and the last clause of the last verse) is divided into five sections. In the semantic-structure analysis of Colossians (Callow and Beekman 1974) it was considered necessary to combine the eight sections of the body into four divisions.

One question still requires further research. While the meaning features of paragraphs, sections, divisions, parts, etc. are essentially the same, the question can be asked: In the surface structure, are there forms which could be considered peculiar to sections, divisions, or parts? For example, in English or Koiné Greek, are there conjunctions peculiar to higher-level units? Probably all that can be said at this stage of research is that no markers peculiar to a higher-level unit are known, but that it would seem reasonable to expect that the boundaries of higher-level units would be clearly marked, i.e., that there would be a greater variety of boundary-marking evidence at the higher levels than would be expected at the boundaries of lower-level units.

10

NARRATIVE UNITS AND THEIR CHARACTERISTICS

10.1 The hierarchy of narrative units

If the paragraph can be considered the typical unit of the nonnarrative genres, then the *episode* would be the corresponding unit in narrative genre. That is to say, all higher units in narrative are like larger versions of the episode in the sense that the episode is the smallest unit in narrative whose constituents are necessarily related to one another by the chronological relations described in chapter 8 (8.4, 8.6, 8.7), principally the stimulus-response group. It is true that occasionally some of the constituents of an episode are more developed and can be analyzed in terms of the stimulus-response relations, but this is not an essential feature. With the episode it is essential; so the episode is characteristically a unit of narration.

A typical episode can be described as a combination of propositional clusters which are related to one another mainly by the stimulus-response relations. It is also a chronological sequence of events which takes place in a single location and a single time span, and which involves a major participant and usually at least one other participant. It is characterized by the semantic features of unity, coherence, and prominence.

Consider, for example, Acts 19:23–41, which is an episode in the book of Acts. It takes place in a single location, Ephesus; there is no lapse in continuity of time; there is a major participant, Paul; and at least three secondary participants are introduced (Demetrius and his fellow silversmiths, the "assembly," and the city clerk).

A *scene* is a combination of episodes with events occurring at a single location or in a spatial trajectory that functions as if it were a single location. There is usually a single major participant throughout. Acts 19:23–21:16 constitutes a scene consisting of six episodes: 19:23–41; 20:1–12; 20:13–38; 21:1–6; 21:7–14; and 21:15–16. As a travel scene, the location is a trajectory; and except for the first episode, Paul is the major participant throughout.

An *act* is a grouping of scenes. Its features of unity, coherence, and prominence contrast with those of other acts. If a narrative is a long work with more levels, then additional units may be introduced as needed.

Just as a paragraph may have constituents which are either propositional clusters or propositions, so also may the episode. However, the episode appears to be somewhat more flexible within the hierarchy than the paragraph, so that a long episode is sometimes best analyzed as consisting of paragraphs, as well as propositional clusters.

An example of this is the long episode of Acts 19:23–41 mentioned above. It is analyzed as consisting of four constituents with the following roles:

Preview (i.e., this episode has a separable Introduction) (23)
Occasion (24–27)
Problem (28–34)
Resolution (35–41)

Each constituent, except the Preview, is probably best analyzed as a paragraph.

10.2 Coherence features in narration

Basically, those features of referential and structural coherence that were discussed for expository and hortatory discourse are applicable also to narrative materials. There will be lexical items from a common semantic or experiential domain and repetitions of participant reference and of certain activities.

There will be chiastic structures, sandwich structures, parallelisms, etc. Since much of narrative is based upon progression and stimulus-response, there will also be the feature of expected chronological and logical sequence. In other words, collocationally, we would not expect a statement about a man climbing a ladder to be followed by a statement such as "And then he pulled in a net full of fish."

Of particular relevance in a narrative is the time and location of the episode. A chain of stimuli and responses are joined together because they are actions that involve the same participants, occur at the same place, and happen during a single period of time and within the same general set of circumstances. Therefore, whenever there is a change in time or place or participants, this often indicates a break within the chain and indicates the start of a new unit at one level or another.

The sandwich structure (inclusio) is a device found in narrative as well as nonnarrative. Frequently, both the form and content are identical or nearly so. The sandwich structure not only provides a quality of completeness, of having gone full circle from the beginning of the unit to the end, but it may also point to the information that is prominent. Keep in mind, however, that the sandwich structure is not a foolproof criterion for boundaries of units. Every time a repetition is noted in the story, it is not necessarily a sandwich structure. There needs to be the convergence of more evidence than duplication of the choice of words.

Opening or closing parallelism is different from a sandwich structure. Parallelism occurs when a particular phrase or clause repeats an earlier occurrence of the same or similar one to draw attention to the boundary of a different unit. The parallelism may be in form, content, or both. Thus, if one paragraph begins with a particular construction and content, that construction and content may be later used to signal the beginning of another paragraph. Similarly, if a paragraph ends with a particular construction and content, that construction and content may be later used to signal the end of another paragraph. This kind of repetition of information is quite different from that of the sandwich structure, where the parallel occurrences of material would signal the opening and closing of the *same* unit, not the opening or the closing of different ones.

10.3 Prominence in narrative

10.3.1 General considerations

Since every semantic unit, in whatever genre, has the meaning feature of prominence, it follows that episodes and higher-level units, right up to the discourse itself, are characterized by prominence. But there are distinctive aspects to narrative that require some further discussion of prominence beyond what has already been described in connection with the paragraph.

First, in speaking of prominence in narrative, a distinction needs to be drawn between a précis and a theme. It would be a relatively simple matter to give a *précis*, which is a brief retelling of the narrative events with no attempt to account for anything but the events in the order in which they appear in the original work. When, however, one searches for the author's *theme*, there is the need to discover the central ideas and theses at various hierarchical levels in the composition. These indicate the author's organization of the events. In stating themes for a narrative, it is important that the logical relationship of the units, not just their chronological sequence, be made apparent.

In analyzing expository and hortatory discourse, natural prominence has been distinguished from marked prominence. It has been found, with consistent results, that a clarified statement is naturally more prominent than what clarifies it; that a statement or command is naturally more prominent than its grounds; that effects are naturally more prominent than causes. These observations hold true unless some special device is used by the author to indicate a different relative prominence. The use of such a device is spoken of as marked prominence. It represents a departure from the normal, natural prominence among the different roles. Something similar is found among the roles in narrative (and dialogue) discourse.

Narration is characterized by a chaining of stimulus-response pairs in which the response of one pair becomes the stimulus of the next. An episode may consist of a single chain which continues until the final response. Others may be considerably more complex consisting of a "chain of chains." Figure 8.19, which gives the relational structure of Acts 3:1–10, illustrates this well. The major chain is setting (3:1)—problem (3:2)—RESOLUTION/occasion (3:3–8)—OUTCOME (3:9–10). But note that both the RESOLUTION/occasion (3:3–8) and the main OUTCOME (3:9–10) consist of stimulus-response chains themselves.

Since the final response in a chain usually represents the Resolution or Outcome to the story, there is a movement from the information with lesser prominence to that with more prominence or significance, from the standpoint of the author's purpose. The statement of the theme for such units would come from the Resolution or Outcome, together with whatever information from the Problem or Occasion that needs to be stated in order that the statement of the Resolution or Outcome makes sense. The final response(s) of an episode are thus the most prominent units within the episode. However, each response in a stimulus-response chain is naturally prominent relative to its stimulus. Further, it is not uncommon for a unit with a stimulus or response role in an episode to consist of a stimulus-response pairing. For example, in the semantic-structure analysis of Mark 2:13–17 (figure 10.1), the Setting contains Jesus' Proposal to Levi, and Levi's Execution of that Proposal. The Execution

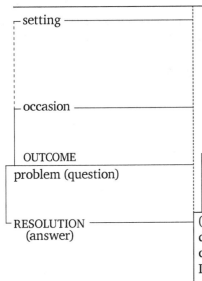

setting	(2:13:14) Jesus went out of the town again to the lakeside. The whole crowd came to him, and he taught them. As he was walking along, he saw Levi, the son of Alphaeus, sitting in the tax collector's booth. Jesus said to him, "Follow me." He got up and followed Jesus.
occasion	(2:15) While Jesus was eating in Levi's house, many tax collectors and sinners were eating with him and his diciples, for there were many who followed him.
OUTCOME problem (question)	(2:16) When the scribes and Pharisees saw that he was eating with sinners and tax collectors, they said to his disciples, "Why does he eat with tax collectors and sinners?"
RESOLUTION (answer)	(2:17) Jesus heard what they asked and said to them: "The healthy do not need a doctor; it is those who are sick who need a doctor, I came in order that I might call sinners: I did not come in order that I might call the righteous."

Figure 10.1. Display of Mark 2:13–17.

is naturally prominent relative to the proposal, so that, within the unit with the role of Setting, the event "he followed Jesus" is (naturally) prominent. (For the natural prominence patterns of the stimulus-response relations, see the chart of communication relations (pp. 112–113).)

In the analysis of Acts 28:7–10 (figure 8.18), 28:10 was analyzed as the Outcome of that unit, and 28:8 and 9 as the Occasion which gave rise to it. A possible theme statement for this unit would be "Paul healed many of the islanders; the outcome was that they honored and resupplied Paul and those with him." (Cf. Blood and Blood 1979:30.) Notice two things about this theme statement: (1) It is expressed in terms of the stimulus-response roles, not the cause-effect roles (e.g., *Because* Paul had healed…), since this is narrative genre; (2) it is necessary to include information from both the Occasion and the Outcome.

Consider also the theme derivation for Mark 2:13–17 (figure 10.1). The last response is the Resolution, but it is incomprehensible apart from much of the information given in the Problem, so the main information in both will appear in the theme statement. This gives rise to the theme statement: "When the Pharisees criticized Jesus for eating with social outcasts, Jesus replied by saying that he had come to call such people."

There are, however, episodes which are more complex than the examples just given. For example, there are those which have two Outcomes, one of which appears approximately in the middle of the sequence of events and the other occurs finally. It would seem that such a phenomenon would cause difficulty in determining which of the two Outcomes is of greater prominence. An example occurs in Mark 1:40–45 (Larson 1979:54). Verses 1:40–42 close with a Resolution, or Outcome, to the request made by the leper for healing. Then follows another three-verses in which Jesus makes a Proposal, the leper disobeys, and a final Outcome is stated. Here we have two paragraphs in sequence within an episode, the first of which, with its Outcome, is analyzed as serving as the Occasion for the second. The second is, therefore, considered to have the greater prominence and, from the content of the final Outcome, it seems that the author's intention at this stage in the development of the discourse is to show the popularity of Jesus and the interest of the people to seek him out for assistance and teaching.

Another type of complexity arises when an episode has both a Resolution and an Outcome. This is a more difficult problem, but the work done on Mark's Gospel, where this type of episode is not uncommon, would appear to suggest that both the Resolution and the Outcome should be regarded as prominent, and included in the theme statement.

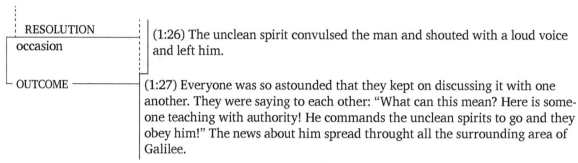

RESOLUTION / occasion	(1:26) The unclean spirit convulsed the man and shouted with a loud voice and left him.
OUTCOME	(1:27) Everyone was so astounded that they kept on discussing it with one another. They were saying to each other: "What can this mean? Here is someone teaching with authority! He commands the unclean spirits to go and they obey him!" The news about him spread throught all the surrounding area of Galilee.

Figure 10.2. Thematic units of Mark 1:21–28

Consider, for example, the last two main constituents of Mark 1:21–28 (figure 10.2). The question arises: Where is the most prominent information to be found in this episode? The answer is based upon a general observation and a particular one:

1. The question can be asked: If 1:27 is the Outcome, what is the Occasion to which it is the response? The information in the Outcome makes it clear that the Occasion comprises the whole episode, and particularly the Resolution, which is the most prominent part of the episode up to that point. So the Outcome communicates the most prominent information.
2. This is confirmed by a sandwich structure. Within the Setting (1:21–22) is the statement: "The people were astonished at the way Jesus taught, because he was teaching them with authority." The reference to "teaching with authority" forms a sandwich structure with 1:27b. There is also the double reference to the people's astonishment (*ekplēssomai* 'be astonished' in 1:22, *thambeomai* 'be astounded' in 1:27). So prominence is being given to Jesus' authority and to the people's astonishment.

The theme statement, then, will be derived primarily from the Outcome, but since this is a response to the Problem and its Resolution, some information is also needed from the units with these two roles. This gives: "When Jesus expelled an unclean spirit from a man, the people were astonished at the authority that he had." This analysis is confirmed by the fact that the theme of the major Gospel constituent 1:14–8:30 is "Jesus shows his authority and power" (Larson 1979:45).

It would seem, then, that when an episode ends with both a Resolution and an Outcome, the most prominent information is the Outcome. However, since the Outcome is a response to the incident as a whole, especially to the Problem and the Resolution, the theme statement will also include information from the Problem and the Resolution; but this information will be given lesser prominence than that from the Outcome. Then, within the units with these roles, other evidence needs to be sought to indicate which information in those units is the most prominent. For example, Larson (1979:51) suggests that the direct quotation form used in 1:27 gives prominence to the information it communicates.

10.3.2 Comparing prominence in narrative and nonnarrative material

If the structure of a narrative is displayed using the same principles as for nonnarrative, i.e., the most prominent information is furthest to the left, its configuration is quite different from that of expository or hortatory discourse. Consider, for example, the display of Mark 2:13–17 (figure 10.1). Generally, the final event(s) represent the prominent information which will be central in formulating a statement of theme. In hortatory and expository discourse, the information most commonly flows in the opposite direction; i.e., it usually begins at the extreme left and moves farther and farther to the right while intermittently returning to a position toward the left, where again it begins moving to the right. Of course, narrative can begin with an Outcome, and exposition can move from support material toward a head; so the above statements are not to be interpreted as absolutes.

In hortatory and expository discourse, *topics* are brought into focus either naturally or by some special marking device. In narrative, it is *participants* who are brought into focus either naturally or through some special device. In nonnarrative discourse, a distinction can be drawn between major, secondary, and minor topics; in narrative discourse, a similar distinction can be seen among major, secondary, and minor participants. When stating the theme of an episode or paragraph within an episode, it is significant to know the status of each of the participants since their level of focus will determine whether or not they will be included as part of the theme statement. Also, in the process of translation, the same relative rank for the various participants needs to be maintained as they appear in an episode or combination of episodes.

Moreover, the maintenance of proper participant focus is not totally dissimilar to the maintenance of topic. In the process of translating narrative material, it is important to know how participants are introduced into a story, how they are referred to after their initial introduction, how they are reintroduced should they leave the story and reappear later on, and how they are phased out of the story.

10.3.3 The prominence features of climax and peak

Up to this point, no mention has been made of climax, even though this is a characteristic of narration which is given careful treatment in books on rhetoric. Is climax a unit of narrative structure or is it rather a prominence device which may be associated with a unit of narrative? If the latter, is there a particular unit with which it is regularly associated?

Climax is generally associated with the buildup of *tension* in plot narratives. Frequently, the tension begins with a statement of the problem which then becomes more entangled and involved as complications to that problem are introduced. The climax would occur at the point where the tension is the greatest and the release of that tension begins—i.e., at the *turning point*. That point is often associated with special grammatical signals (see Longacre 1974:217–228). This surface-structure phenomenon is referred to as the (grammatical) *peak*.

There is a close connection between the peak and the climax of a story. The signals associated with the peak are not drawing attention to the units in which they occur; that is, they do not indicate that those units have higher significance or prominence. Rather, this device is similar to the use of contrast that may be found in the work of an artist. The artist may paint a scene showing the winds and torrential rains with the lightning flashing across the sky and then have a bird perched on a branch of a swaying tree with a small twig in its mouth to depict peace. The contrast to the raging storm highlights and gives prominence to the notion of peace. When suspense and tension build up in a narrative with various grammatical and rhetorical signals contributing to that suspense, these serve to point ahead toward the resolution, giving it a greater significance and prominence by virtue of the contrast. In other words, the greater the problem and the more involved the complications, the more significant the resolution, regardless of how simple and straightforward it may be in itself.

It follows, then, from this description of peak and climax, that the climax is a feature of prominence that is most often signaled in surface structure by special devices collectively referred to as the grammatical peak. The function of climax is to draw attention to and to highlight the Resolution unit of the discourse or part of the discourse in which it occurs. However, it does not follow that every Resolution is associated with a climax. A Resolution is only described as climactic if it is marked by a peak, thus highlighting the Resolution by contrast.

It should be noted that this understanding of peak is different from our understanding of prominence signals in expository or hortatory material. There we expect and find that an information span which is not naturally prominent may be marked so that it becomes at least of equal prominence with the information that is naturally prominent. In narrative, the special rhetorical and grammatical prominence signals tend to be found mainly in the units dealing with the problem and its complications. Yet, they do not attract prominence to those units themselves. Rather, they point more forcefully and more meaningfully to the resolution.

10.4 The purpose of narrative units

It has been frequently claimed that it is easier to determine the theme of expository or hortatory discourse than it is to determine the theme of narrative discourse. Such is the case because in narration the author communicates his meaning less directly through the events which he reports. Nevertheless, there should be no markedly greater difficulty in determining the theme of narrative discourse than there is in determining the theme of nonnarrative. However, if one attempts to identify the author's purpose for narrative discourse, it must be granted that the task is more difficult. This is because the derivation of theme is based upon objective evidence that is available in the text, whereas the identification of the purpose requires that the thematic content of the discourse be carefully examined in the light of a detailed understanding of the communication situation in which it was given. When a narrative occurs within a larger discourse (e.g., Gal. 1:13–2:21 or the various episodes that occur within groupings of episodes in the Gospels), then much of the needed information for identifying the purpose is retrievable from the context. When, however, there is no explicit context, the task of identifying the author's purpose becomes much more difficult—not impossible, but difficult. The analyst must search for clues. Some will come from the thematic content, some from the situational meaning features throughout the discourse, and some from extra-textual indications of both the specific and general situation in which the discourse was given. All of these will contribute to the identification of the purpose.

10.5 The time-line

It has been stressed at a number of points in this theory that narrative is based upon a sequence of events in the referential world of the discourse. The same is true of the stimulus-response relations—every response follows every stimulus in the time of the referential world. Many languages mark this succession of events with various surface-structure devices—special affixes on the verb, absence of subject phrases, tenses used, special particles, even tone. This succession of events in time is often referred to as the *time-line*.

Various questions naturally arise in this connection:

1. How is the time-line signaled in the New Testament narratives? How did a reader know that event B followed event A? Are there differences between one New Testament author and another in this respect?
2. How does the time-line relate to the plot structure which characterizes most of the narrative units? Of course, it indicates that the various plot roles follow each other in time; but is that all it does? How is the time-line related to the phenomenon of peak? Are there any signals on the time-line that indicate (say) the start of the Resolution, which is the climax of the story?

Some answers are beginning to emerge to the questions grouped under number 1. As might be expected, the aorist tense is the tense commonly used on the time-line, but in Mark's Gospel, for example, the "historical present" is also used for this purpose. But the significance of such tenses as the imperfect and the perfect is by no means fully understood. The imperfect, for example, is not uncommon in Settings, where the information is of lower prominence, yet it is also used in Luke's summaries in Acts, from which thematic material is derived. It seems clear, too, that the conjunctions *kai* 'and' and *de* 'and, but' have a grouping function for time-line events, but they are used differently by different authors. Greek also has a choice between the finite verb and the participle for time-line events—what does this distinction signal?

While, then, it is held that the stimulus-response roles are more important from a semantic perspective than the time-line, since they describe what function each information unit has in the narrative, nevertheless the time-line is also an integral part of the structure of narrative, and therefore needs to be understood and its significance described within the overall context of a theory of semantic structure.

References

[*NOT = Notes on Translation* published by SIL International 1962–2001. Discontinued.]

Alston, William P. 1968. "Meaning and Use". In Parkinson.

Austin, J. 1962. *How to Do Things with Words.* New York: Oxford University Press.

Author unknown. 1975. "On Contextual Unity". *NOT* 56:42.

Bach, Emmon. 1971. "Questions". *Linguistic Inquiry* II:153–166.

Baker, C. 1970. "Notes on the Description of English Questions". *Foundations of Language* 6:197–219.

Ballard, D.Lee. 1973. "On the Translation of Greek Relationals". *NOT* 47:18–21.

Barnwell, Katharine. 1973. "Systematic Grammar—An Approach to Meaning". *SIL Papers on Semantics and Discourse.* Huntington Beach, CA: Summer Institute of Linguistics.

Barnwell, Katharine. 1980. *Introduction to Semantics and Translation.* Horsleys Green, England: Summer Institute of Linguistics.

Baxter, J. Sidlow. 1973. *Explore the Book.* Grand Rapids, Michigan: Zondervan.

Bee, Darlene L. 1973. *Neo-Tagmemics: An Integrated Approach to Linguistic Analysis and Description.* Edited by Alan Healey and Doreen Marks. Ukarumpa, Papua New Guinea: Summer Institute of Linguistics.

Beekman, John. 1967. "Introduction to Skewing of the Lexical and Grammatical Hierarchies". *NOT* 23:1.

Beekman, John. 1970a. "Propositions and Their Relations Within a Discourse". *NOT* 37:6–23.

Beekman, John. 1970b. "A Structural Display of Propositions in Jude". *NOT* 37:27–31.

Beekman, John. 1970c. "Structural Notes on the Book of Jude (1)". *NOT* 37:36–38.

Beekman, John, ed. 1972. "Analyzing and Translating the Questions of the New Testament". *NOT* 44:3–21.

Beekman, John, and John Callow. 1974. *Translating the Word of God.* Grand Rapids, Michigan: Zondervan.

Bendor-Samuel, Pam. 1976. "Titus: Analysis of the Larger Semantic Units". *NOT* 61:2–8.

Betts, La Vera. 1971. "The Parintintin World View". *NOT* 41:16, 17.

Black, Max. 1968. *The Labrinth of Language.* London: Pall Mall.

Blight, Richard C. 1970. "An Aternate Display of Jude". *NOT* 37:32–36.

Blight, Richard C. 1977. *A Literary-Semantic Analysis of Paul's First Discourse to Timothy.* Prepublication draft. John Beekman, General Editor.

Blood, David L., and Doris E. Blood. 1979. Overview of Acts. *NOT* 74:2—36.

Boucher, Madeleine. 1977. *The Mysterious Parable: A Literary Study.* The Catholic Biblical Quarterly, Monograph Series 6. Washington, D.C.: The Catholic Biblical Association of America.

Brennan, Paul. 1968. *The Structure of Koiné Greek Narrative.* Ann Arbor: University Microfilms International.

Brooks, Cleanth, and Robert Penn Warren. 1958. *Modern Rhetoric.* 2nd ed. New York: Harcourt, Brace.

Bush, Charles D. 1973. "Fundamentals of Junction Grammar". Unpublished, mimeographed, evaluation edition, Brigham Young University, Provo, Utah.

Buth, Randall John. 1976. An "Introductory Study of the Paragraph Structure of Biblical Hebrew Narrative". Master's thesis, The American Institute of Holy Land Studies.

Buth, Randall John. 1976. "Mark's Use of *Palin* and Its Relationship to Discourse and Plot Analysis". *NOT* 61:32–36.

Butler, Inez M. 1967. "Use of Third Person for First Person in the Gospel of John". *NOT* 26:10–14.

Callow, John. 1970. "Structural Notes on the Book of Jude (2)". *NOT* 37:38–41.

Callow, John. 1977. "The Semantic Relation of Manner–A Reconsideration of Its Status". *NOT* 63:23–26.

Callow, John, and John Beekman. 1974. *An Analysis of the Semantic Structure of the Epistle to the Colossians.* Prepublication draft. Mimeographed.

Callow, Kathleen. 1970. "More on Propositions and Their Relations Within a Discourse". *NOT* 37:23–27.

Callow, Kathleen, Philip Hewer, and Tony Naden. 1975. *A Propositional Grammar Outline: A Format for the Presentation and Comparison of Grammatical Systems*. Ghana: Institute of Linguistics.

Carnap, Rudolf. 1958. *Introduction to Symbolic Logic and Its Applications*. New York: Dover.

Chafe, Wallace L. 1970. *Meaning and the Structure of Language*. Chicago: The University of Chicago Press.

Culley, Robert C. 1974. "Interpretation-Structural Analysis: Is It Done with Mirrors?" *Interpretation* 28:165–181.

Currier, Constance Elizabeth. 1977. "Participant Reference in Bahasa Indonesia Narrative Discourse". Master's thesis, The University of Texas at Arlington.

Deibler, Ellis W., Jr. 1969. "Basic Structure: 1 Corinthians". *NOT* 31:34–39.

Deibler, Ellis W., Jr. 1973. "The Relationship of Propositions to Sentences". *SIL Papers on Semantics and Discourse*. Mimeographed. Huntington Beach, CA: Summer Institute of Linguistics.

Deibler, Ellis W., Jr. 1976. *Semantic Relations of Gahuku Verbs*. SIL Publications in Linguistics and Related Fields, Publication 48, Chapter 6.

Duff, Martha. 1973. "Contrastive Features of Written and Oral Texts in Amuesha". *NOT* 50:2–13.

Elliot, D. 1971. "The Grammar of Emotive and Exclamatory Sentences in English". *Working Papers in Linguistics* 8. Columbus: Ohio State University.

Erickson, Frederick David. 1971. "The Cycle of Situational Frames: A Model for Microethnography in Urban Anthropology". Paper read at the Midwest Anthropology Meeting, Detroit, Michigan, April 30, 1971. Mimeographed.

Fillmore, Charles J. 1968. "The Case for Case". *Universals in Linguistics Theory*. Edited by Emmon Bach and Robert T. Harms. New York: Holt, Tinehart, and Winston.

Fleming, Ilah. 1973. "Techniques for Semological Analysis". *SIL Papers on Semantics and Discourse*. Mimeographed. Huntington Beach, CA: Summer Institute of Linguistics.

Fleming, Ilah. 1978. *Field Guide for Communication Situation, Semantic and Morphemic Analysis*. Prepublication draft. Dallas, TX: Summer Institute of Linguistics.

Forbes, John. 1854. *Symmetrical structure of Scripture: Or, the principles of Scripture parallelism, exemplified in an analysis of the Decalogue, the Sermon on the Mount, and other passages of the sacred writings*. Edinburgh: T. & T. Clark.

Fortune, David. 1976. "Indigenous Writing Styles as Related to Discourse Analysis". *NOT* 59:17f.

Foster-Harris. 1959. *The Basic Patterns of Plot*. Norman: University of Oklahoma Press.

Frantz, Donald. 1968. "Translation and Underlying Structure I: Relations". *NOT* 30:22–28.

Frantz, Donald. 1970. "Translation and Underlying Structure II. Pronominalization and Reference". *NOT* 38:3–10.

Frantz, Donald. 1973. "Generative Semantics". *SIL Papers on Semantics and Discourse*. Mimeographed. Huntington Beach, CA: Summer Institute of Linguistics.

Frantz, Donald. 1974a. "Speech Acts and Sentence Types". *North America Branch, Technical Bulletin* 14:1–5.

Frantz, Donald. 1974b. "Illocutionary Force in Generative Semantics". *North America Branch, Technical Bulletin* 17:1–4.

Fuglesang, Andres. 1973. *Applied Communication in Developing Countries, Ideas and Observations*. Uppsala: Dag Hammarskjoeld Foundation.

Fuller, Daniel P. 1959. *Inductive Method of Bible Study*. Chapter 7, "The Problem of the Narrative Form". Pasadena, CA: Fuller Theological Seminary.

Fuller, Daniel P. 1967. "Delimiting and Interpreting the Larger Literary Units". *NOT* 28:1–12.

Fuller, Daniel P. 1969. "Hermeneutics". Unpublished typewritten ms. Pasadena, CA.

Fuller, Daniel P. 1973. "Analysis of Romans 11:11–32". *NOT* 48:2–4.

Gordon, D., and G. Lakoff. 1971. "Conversation Postulates". *Chicago Linguistics Society* 7:63–84.

Green, G. 1973. "How to Get People to Do Things with Words". *Some New Directions in Linguistics*. Edited by Robert W. Shuy. Washington: Georgetown University.

Greenwood, David. 1970. "Rhetorical Criticism and *Formeschichte*: Some Methodological Considerations". *Journal of Biblical Literature* 89:418–426.

Grimes, Joseph E. 1975. *The Thread of Discourse*. Janua Linguarum Studia Memoriae Nicolai van Wijk Dedicata. Series Minor 207. Edited by C. H. van Schooneveld. The Hague: Mouton.

Gutt, Ernst-August. 1973. "Structural Phenomena in the Greek Text of Acts 22:6 in the Light of Discourse Analysis". *NOT* 48:11–23.

Hale, Austin, ed. 1973. *Clause, Sentence, and Discourse Patterns in Selected Languages of Nepal, Part I, General Approach.* Summer Institute of Linguistic Publications in Linguistics and Related Fields, Publication 40. Edited by Irvine Davis. Kathmandu, Nepal: University Press.

Hale, Austin, 1976. In Robert E. Longacre, *An Anatomy of Speech Notations.* PdR Press Publications in Tagmemics 3. Lisse: Peter de Ridder Press.

Hale, Clarence B. 1975. "Paul's Use of *dia touto*". *NOT* 57:2–4.

Halliday, M. A. K. 1973. *Explorations in the Functions of Language.* Explorations in Language Study Series. General Editors: Peter Doughty; Geoffry Thornton; and M. A. K. Halliday. London: Edward Arnold.

Halliday, M. A. K., and Ruqaiya Hasan. 1976. *Cohesion in English.* London: Longman Group Limited.

Headland, Edna. 1975. "Information Load and Layout in Tunebo". *NOT* 58:2–24.

Hendricks, William O. 1973. *Essays on Semiolinguistics and Verbal Art.* The Hague, Paris: Mouton.

Heringer, J. 1972. "Some Grammatical Correlates on Felicity Conditions and Presuppositions". *Working Papers in Linguistics* 11. Columbus: Ohio State University.

Hjelmslev, Louis. 1953. "Prolegomena to a Theory of Language". Translated by Francis Whitfield. *Indiana University Publications in Anthropology and Linguistics*, Memoir 7, of the *International Journal of American Linguistics.*

Holdcraft, David. 1968. "Meaning of Illocutionary Acts". In Parkinson, ed.

Hollenbach, Barbara. 1973a. "A Preliminary Semantic Classification of Temporal Concepts". *NOT* 47:2–8.

Hollenbach, Barbara. 1973b. "Some Further Thoughts on Relations Between Propositions". *NOT* 47:9–11.

Hollenbach, Bruce. 1967. "Some More Relationships in the Material Words". *NOT* 26:6–10.

Hollenbach, Bruce. 1969. "A Method for Displaying Semantic Structure". *NOT* 31:22–34.

Hollenbach, Bruce. 1975. "Discourse Structure, Interpropositional Relations, and Translation". *NOT* 56:2–21.

Holzhausen, Andreas. 1974. "Narratives in the New Testament". *NOT* 53:22–33.

Hunt, Geoffrey R. 1975. "Towards an Analysis of Cause-Effect Relations". *NOT* 58:32–34.

Hunt, Geoffrey R. 1980. "A Logical Development". *Notes on Linguistics* 16:37–40. Dallas, TX Summer Institute of Linguistics.

Hutchinson, L. 1971. "Presupposition and Belief Inferences". *Chicago Linguistic Society.* 7:134–141.

Jebb, John. 1820. *Sacred Literature: Comparing a review of the principles of composition laid down by the late Robert Lowth in his praelections, and Isaiah: and an application of the principles so reviewed, to the illustration of the New Testament; in a series of critical observations on the style and structure of that sacred volume.* London: Cadell and Davies.

Jensen, Irving L. 1963. *Independent Bible Study.* Chicago: Moody Press.

Johnson, Linda, and Richard Bayless. 1976. "Cohesion in a Discourse-Based Linguistic Theory". University of Michigan. Ms.

Jones, Linda Kay. 1977. *Theme in English Expository Discourse.* Edward Sapir Monograph Series in Language, Culture, and Cognition 2. Lake Bluff, IL: Jupiter Press.

Joos, Martin. 1957. Meaning in relation to MT. In Léon Dostert (ed.), *Report of the Eighth Annual Round Table Meeting on Linguistics and Language Studies: Research in machine translation,* Washington, D.C., April 12-13, 1957. Washington, D.C.: Georgetown University Press. (https://repository.library.georgetown.edu/bitstream/handle/10822/555452/GURT_1957.pdf)

Joos, Martin. 1958. "Semology: A Linguistic Theory of Meaning". *Studies in Linguistics* 13:3–4:53–70.

Karn, Gloria Jean. 1976. "Tuyuca Plot Structure—A Pilot Study". M.A. thesis. The University of Texas at Arlington.

Kingston, Peter K. E. 1973. "Repetition as a Feature of Discourse Structure in Mamainde". *NOT* 50:13–22.

Kinsler, F. Ross. 1972. *An Inductive Study of the Book of Mark.* n.p.: William Carey Library.

Kopesec, Michael F. 1978. "Preliminary Observations on the Genre of Mark and Some Implications for Discourse Analysis". Unpublished paper. Dallas, TX

Lakoff, George. 1970. *Irregularity in Syntax.* New York: Holt, Rinehart, and Winston.

Landerman, Peter, and Donald Frantz. 1972. *Notes on Grammatical Theory.* Lima, Peru: Summer Institute of Linguistics and Ministry of Education of Peru. Mimeographed.

Langendoen, D. Terence. 1969. *The Study of Syntax.* New York: Holt, Rinhart, and Winston.

Langendoen, D. Terence. 1970. *Essentials of English Grammar.* Tokyo: Taishukan.

Larkin, D., and M. O'Malley. 1973. "Declarative Sentences and the Rule-of-Conversation Hypothesis". *Chicago Linguistics Society* 9:306–319.

Larson, Mildred L. 1965. A "Method for Checking Discourse Structure in Bible Translation". *NOT* 17.

Larson, Mildred L. 1979. "The Gospel of Mark, 1:1–3:6". *The Semantic Structure of Written Communication*, Part 3. Ms. Dallas, TX.

Lee, Robert, and Carolyn Lee. 1975. "An Analysis of the Larger Semantic Units of I Thessalonians". *NOT* 56:23–40.

Lithgow, David. 1971. "Change of Subject in Muyuw". *NOT* 41:21–27.

Longacre, Robert E. 1972. "Some Implications of Deep and Surface Structure Analysis for Translation". *NOT* 45:2–10.

Longacre, Robert E. 1973. "Hierarchy on the Contemporary Linguistic Scene". *SIL Papers on Semantics and Discourse.* Mimeographed. Huntington Beach, CA: Summer Institute of Linguistics.

Longacre, Robert E. 1976. *An Anatomy of Speech Notions.* PdR Press Publications in Tagmemics 3, Lisse, The Netherlands: Peter de Ridder Press.

Longacre, Robert E. 1980. *The Grammar of Discourse.* Prepublication draft. Dallas, TX.

Lowe, Ivan. 1973. "Group Theory for the Consumer with Applications to Pronominal Reference, Deictics, Conversation and Discourse". *SIL Papers on Semantics and Discourse.* Mimeographed. Huntington Beach, CA: Summer Institute of Linguistics.

Manabe, Takashi. 1974. "Surface Structure Characteristics of the Beginnings of Paragraphs and Discourses in Luke". *NOT* 54:26.

Manabe, Takashi. 1978. "Topic-Comment Based Linguistics Model and Its Application to Greek and Japanese". *Reading in Semantics.* Vol. 3. Research Papers of the Texas SIL at Dallas. Dallas, TX: Summer Institute of Linguistics.

McCawley, N. 1973. "Boy! Is Syntax Easy!" *Chicago Linguistic Society* 9:369–377.

Merrifield, William R. 1973a. "Case Grammar." *SIL Papers on Semantics and Discourse.* Huntington Beach, CA. Summer Institute of Linguistics.

Merrifield, William R. 1972. "Doublets". *NOT* 43:3–34.

Merrifield, William R. 1973b. "Semantic Components as Geometric Planes". *NOT* 49:18–21.

Miller, George A. 1956. The magical number seven, plus or minus two: Some limits on our capacity for processing information. *Psychological Review* 63(2):81-97.

Moore, Bruce R. 1972. Doublets. *NOT* 1(43):3—34.

Moulton, Richard G. 1905. *The Literary Study of the Bible.* London: lbisler.

Muilenberg, James. 1969. "Form Criticism and Beyond". *Journal of Biblical Literature* 88:1–18.

Newman, Bonnie. 1975. "Emphasis and Its Relevance to Longuda Translation". *NOT* 57:4–11.

Nida, Eugene A. 1975. *Componential analysis of meaning: An introduction to semantic structures.* The Hague, The Netherlands: Mouton Publishers

Parkinson, H. A. R., ed. 1968. *The Theory of Meaning.* London: Oxford University Press.

Perrin, Norman. 1969. *What is Redaction Criticism?* Guides to Biblical Scholarship: New Testament Series. Philadelphia: Fortress Press.

Pickering, Wilbur Norman. 1977. *A Framework for Discourses Analysis.* Ph.D. dissertation. University of Toronto.

Pike, Eunice V. 1967. "Skewing of the Lexical and Grammatical Hierarchy as it Affects Translation". *NOT* 23:1–3.

Pike, Kenneth L. 1959. "Language as Particle, Wave, and Field." *The Texas Quarterly* 2:37–54. Reprinted in *K. L. Pike: Selected Writings* ed. by Ruth Brend, 1973.

Pike, Kenneth L., and Evelyn G Pike. 1974. *Grammatical Analysis.* Norman, OK: Summer Institute of Linguistics.

Roberts, Edgar V. 1973. *Writing Themes about Literature.* 3rd ed. Englewood Cliffs, N. J.: Prentice-Hall.

Ross, J. 1970. "On Declarative Sentences". *Readings in English Transformational Grammar.* Edited by Roderick A. Jacobs and Peters. Rosenbaum. Boston, MA: Wiley.

Ruskin, John. 1947. The form and power of Holy Scripture. In Howard Tillman Kuist (ed.), *These words upon thy heart: Scripture and the Christian response.* Richmond, VA: John Knox Press.

Russell, Robert L. 1969. "Discourse Analysis and Bible Translation: A Few Suggestions". *NOT* 31:40–43.

Ryken, Leland. 1974. *The Literature of the Bible*. Grand Rapids, MI: Zondervan.

Sadock, J. 1969. "Whimperatives". *Studies Presented to Robert B. Lees by His Students*. Edited by J. Sadock and Vanek. Edmonton, Canada: Linguistic Research.

Sadock, J. 1971. "Queclaratives". *Chicago Linguistic Society* 7:223–231.

Sadock, J. 1972. "Speech Act Idioms". *Chicago Linguistic Society* 8:329–339.

Saumjan, S. K. 1965. "Outline of the Applicational Generative Model for the Description of Language". *Foundations of Language*, 1:3, 189–222.

Searle, J. R. 1969. *Speech Acts*. Cambridge, England: Cambridge University Press.

Sheffler, Margaret. 1969. "Result of Network Diagramming: As applied to the revision of Munduruku Mark". *NOT* 32.

Shwayder, D. S. 1968. "Uses of Language and Uses of Word". In Parkinson, ed.

Smith, Donald K., Daniel R. Brewster, and Alice L. Brewster. 1974. *Creating a Living Translation*. Eugene, OR and Nairobi, Kenya: Daystar. Mimeographed.

Spivey, Robert A. April, 1974. "Interpretation-Structuralism and Biblical Studies: The Uninvited Guest". *Interpretation*.

Spradley, James P. 1972. Foundations of cultural knowledge. In James P. Spradley (ed.), *Culture and cognition: Rules, maps and plans*. San Francisco, CA: Chandler.

Starobinski, Jean. 1971. "An Essay on Literary Analysis—Mark 5:1–20". *The Ecumenical Review*, October 1971, 377–397.

Suharno, lgnatious, and Kenneth L. Pike, eds. 1976. *From Baudi to Indonesian, Studies in Linguistics*. Irian Jaya: Regions Press. Published by Cenderawasih University and Summer Institute of Linguistics.

Talbert, Charles H. 1966. "A Non-Pauline Fragment at Romans 3:24–26?" *Journal of Biblical Literature* 85:287–296.

Thomas, David, and John Daly, eds. 1974. *1974 Work Papers*, Vol. 18. Grand Forks, N.D.: Summer Institute of Linguistics. Mimeographed.

Thomas, David. 1972. "Comments on Sentences, Propositions and Notes on Translation 37". NOT 45:11–14.

Thomas, David, ed. 1973. *1973 Work Papers*. Vol. 17. Mimeographed. Grand Forks, ND: Summer Institute of Linguistics.

Thomas, David, 1975a. "Paragraph Analysis of the Parable of the Pounds". *NOT* 56:22–28.

Thomas, David, 1975b. "Location and Participant Bracketing in Matthew". *NOT* 58:32–34.

Trail, Ronald L. 1973. "Patterns in Clause, Sentence, and Discourse in Selected Languages of India and Nepal. Part I, Sentence and Discourse". Final Report Contract No. OEC-0-9-97721-2778(014). Institute of International Studies, U. S. Department of Health, Education, and Welfare. Norman, OK: Summer Institute of Linguistics, University of Oklahoma.

Traina, Robert A. 1952. *Methodical Bible Study*. Wilmore, KY: By the author, Asbury Theological Seminary.

Van Dijk, Teun A. 1977a. Semantic macro-structures and knowledge frames in discourse comprehension. In Marcel Adam Just and Patricia A. Carpenter (eds.), *Cognitive processes in comprehension*, 3–32. Hillsdale, NJ: Lawrence Erlbaum.

Van Dijk, Teun A. 1977b. *Text and Context*. London and New York: Longman Group.

Via, Daniel O., Jr. 1975. *Kerygma and Comedy in the New Testament: A structuralist approach to hermeneutic*. Philadelphia: Fortress Press.

Wallis, Ethel E. 1971a. "Contrastive Plot Structures of the Four Gospels". *NOT* 40:3–16.

Wallis, Ethel E. 1971b. "Discourse Focus in Mezquital Otomi". *NOT* 45:14–16.

Wallis, Ethel E. 1973. "The Rhetorical Organization of Luke's Discourse". *NOT* 48:5–10.

Waltz, Nathan. 1976. "Discourse Patterns in John 11". *NOT* 59:2–8.

Werner, John R. 1981. "*Hina* Content Clauses." *Selected Techinical Articles Related to Translation* 3:1–25. Dallas, TX: Summer Institute of Linguistics.

Wise, Mary Ruth. 1973. "Some Contributions of Tagmemics to Discourse Studies". *SIL Papers on Semantics and Discourse*. Mimeographed. Huntington Beach, CA: Summer Institute of Linguistics.

Wunderlich, D. 1977. "Assertions, Conditional Speech Acts, and Practical lnferences." *Journal of Pragmatics*. Netherlands: North Holland Publishing.

Young, Richard E., Alton L. Becker, and Kenneth L. Pike. 1970. *Rhetoric, Discovery and Change*. New York: Harcourt, Brace, World.

CPSIA information can be obtained
at www.ICGtesting.com
Printed in the USA
LVHW100234101219
640004LV00009B/470/P

9 781556 714061